100+ IDEAS
FOR TEACHING ENGLISH

CONTINUUM ONE HUNDREDS SERIES

100+ IDEAS
FOR TEACHING
ENGLISH

Angella Cooze

continuum

Continuum International Publishing Group

The Tower Building   80 Maiden Lane, Suite 704
11 York Road   New York, NY 10038
London
SE1 7NX

www.continuumbooks.com

British Library Cataloguing-in-Publication Data
A catalogue record for this book is available from the
British Library.

ISBN: 0–8264–8311–9 (paperback)

Library of Congress Cataloging-in-Publication Data
A catalog record for this book is available from the
Library of Congress.

Typeset by Ben Cracknell Studios
Printed and bound in Great Britain by Ashford Colour Press Ltd,
Gosport, Hampshire

CONTENTS

SECTION 3 Introducing reading and understanding

SECTION 7 **Non-fiction**

SECTION 8 **Speaking and listening**

SECTION 9 **Thinking skills**

SECTION 10 Drama in the English classroom

SECTION 11 ICT and English

SECTION 12 Boys and English

SECTION 13 Differentiation

Let's start at the beginning

The 'learning environment' has been something of a buzz phrase for a number of years. It is, however, more than that. When students walk into your room, they should feel that they have entered:

○ a *classroom*, a place of and for learning;
○ an *English classroom* specifically;
○ *your classroom* in particular.

Establish a clutter-free and organized room. Ensure that desks, tables and shelving are used, mainly, for one purpose. Exercise books, textbooks, novels, paper, pens, dictionaries and worksheets should have a specific place, preferably labelled.

Class displays should be current and well presented. After all, the prime reason for displaying work is to encourage a sense of pride in your pupils. This is difficult to establish with tatty and torn work from pupils who have long since left the school. There is a place for keeping some work as models, but this needs to be made obvious. Display work in headed sections. If possible and appropriate, a considerable proportion should be marked rather than simply showing only pieces of work with little relevance other than as a display piece. This seems like a lot of extra work, but ask for help – some pupils actively enjoy creating displays.

Certain key terms or tips can be displayed prominently in the class. Those that you feel are most important should be displayed on the same wall as the board, as it is in this direction that pupils will be facing most often. Make sure that they are in a clear, large font and that there is some variety in the way in which they are presented. Some may have accompanying visual images or be in the form of a mnemonic, for example. Try to display as many as is practical. Pupils spend a lot of time gazing at walls – lost in thought, or simply lost. You may wish to include key literary terms, vocabulary alternatives for critical essays, simplified level descriptors and common spelling errors. This really is a surprisingly simple and effective way of helping information stick. It also has the added effect of clearly identifying the room as an English classroom.

Pupils' writing is much improved if they can move away from simple one-clause sentences and use a variety of sentence types. Recognizing this variety also sharpens their understanding of text. The following tasks are, in the first instance, concerned with helping pupils to identify different types of sentence (namely simple, compound and complex), and then move into using this recognition to write their own. Some tasks may not be suitable for all levels of ability, so select the level you feel most appropriate.

SIMPLE SENTENCES

Pupils may need to be reminded that a sentence usually contains a subject and a verb. Give each pair of pupils pieces of card printed with either a subject or verb phrase. Each subject should have a matching verb phrase. Pupils then put the pieces together to form sentences. Each pair can read out one of the completed sentences. Explain that these are simple sentences, made of one clause.

COMPOUND SENTENCES

It is useful here if pupils have already looked at connectives/conjunctions as these will be necessary to their understanding. Display to the class pairs of simple sentences which are jumbled up, such as:

I went shopping. The dog was covered in mud.
Richard was great at football. I bought some books.
The sofa was filthy. He was terrible at rugby.

Ask pupils to, firstly, work out which sentences go together. Their next task is to join them together using connectives to make one long sentence. Explain that these are called compound sentences and are made of two clauses, usually joined by a connective, and that each clause could be a sentence on its own.

Out of simple, compound and complex sentences this is the trickiest, but some of the most common patterns can be understood fairly easily. Display for pupils a table such as the one below.

Subject	Extra information	Verb phrase
My uncle John	who is a soldier	is coming to tea.
The crowd	which had been quiet all match	let out a roar.

Read through the table and ask pupils to copy it into their books. Give pupils cards with subordinate clauses written on them. In pairs, ask them to arrange them with their original subject and verb phrase cards to make complex sentences. Ask pupils to read out one of their complex sentences and then add two of these further examples to their tables. Focus the class on how these sentences are formed.

Next, put a series of adverbial sentence openers on the board. Ask the class to complete sentences such as the following:

Although I had always been a vegetarian,
While leaning against the wall minding my own business,

Finally, ask pupils to write one sentence of each type in a short passage about what they did at the weekend. Pupils can then swap their work and identify the sentence types in each other's writing. The important thing to emphasize is that they should use a variety of sentence types in their written work.

Skillful recognition and use of adjectives in writing can enhance pupils' reading and understanding skills as well as their own writing. Give the following information and task to your students. **Adjectives** are words which give us more information about a noun. They **describe** nouns in more detail. For example:

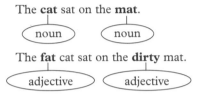

The **cat** sat on the **mat**.

noun   noun

The **fat** cat sat on the **dirty** mat.

adjective   adjective

The adjectives add more information and help create a fuller picture. Now add adjectives to the following sentences.

The boy bought some trousers.
The house was empty.

This sort of exercise can be developed and extended ad infinitum. For example, give pupils passages where the adjectives are left out and ask them to fill in the gaps. Try to get them to think about the effect created. Another exercise is to get pupils to describe something (or someone if you are confident that it will not turn nasty!) by adjective alone. For example, 'I am green, rectangular, chipped and scratched' may describe a classroom door; or 'I am red, white, jolly and fat' may describe Father Christmas. If the class has difficulty with this, allow them to use a set number of other word types to help them along, but maintain the focus on adjectives.

Adjective use is not confined to narrative forms and it is important to instil in your pupils some understanding of how adjectives are used in non-fiction texts, too. An effective and simple way of doing this is by using (real or devised) advertisements, holiday brochures or property descriptions from estate agents. Again, remove the adjectives from the texts and ask pupils to replace them. Get the class to focus on how adjective choices are used as a form of persuasion.

This can be extended by pupils finding some examples of adjective use in everyday life. For example, 'crisp, delicious apples', 'smooth, clear skin' and 'wholesome and filling meals for one' are the sorts of adjective-use they should have easy access to and which lend themselves to discussions about connotation.

Many of the tasks in other sections of this book look at aspects of implied meaning and connotation. Pupils' understanding of layers of meaning is an important aspect of their reading and understanding as well as their own writing. The following suggestions can be used to consolidate work done in other topic areas or as discrete tasks. The stages can be altered or omitted as best suits your class.

Display to the class a list of names of – real or devised – cars or soft drinks. Read through the list with pupils. If you think it appropriate, discuss some of the names, asking pupils for ideas about what is suggested about the car or drink by the name alone. Ask pupils to select three and draw the car or soft-drink container as they think best fits the name. For example, car names may include 'Rat', 'Cougar', 'Matador' or 'Cockroach' and soft drinks may include 'Sprint', 'VitFresh', 'Fizzbomb' or 'Swamp Juice'. The important thing is that the list contains product names which carry implied meaning and associations both negative and positive.

Next, ask pupils to feed back their ideas to the class, looking at the connotations they picked up on from the product name. Note down any images or ideas that are most common or pertinent. Focus the class on the suggestions they have made and what connotations have been evoked by the product name. Ask pupils to identify which names from the list they felt were most and least successful as product names, identifying the connotations of each name and discussing the effects created.

INTRODUCING IMPLIED MEANING

CONNOTATION:

Most pupils will have been familiarized with the parts of speech during Key Stage 2 (KS2). It is, however, a good idea to check their understanding – both to reinforce their learning and to establish the needs of your class. The following can be used as an *aide memoir* or as the foundation for class exercises.

Nouns are naming words. They are used to name things, people or ideas/feelings and are often the most important part of a sentence. Look at the following sentences. Without nouns, it is difficult to make sense of them.

The _____ went to the _____ to get some _____.

_____ is a good _____ for a _____.

Fill in the gaps and see what different sentences you come up with.

There are 3 types of noun:

○ **Concrete nouns** – these name objects you can **see** or **touch**; such as a **book**, a **glove**, a **boy** or a **car**.

○ **Proper nouns** – these name **particular** people, places or things; such as **Paul**, **Leeds**, **America** or **Harry Potter**.

○ **Abstract nouns** – these name **feelings** or **ideas**, such as **anger**, **happiness**, **rest** or **tomorrow**.

Look again at the nouns you chose to fill in the gaps. What type of noun are they?

These activities, and others like them, can be extended and developed as you see fit. For example, short passages can be read and noun types identified in columns or replaced with others of the same type. Or this work can be tied in with other aspects of writing, such as creating narrative, by emphasizing how different noun choices can create very different effects.

It is generally the case that most confusion arises around abstract nouns, so be sure to keep it simple at first. Perhaps get the class to differentiate on the basis of the senses – concrete nouns are experienced through the senses while abstract nouns are not.

An understanding of pronouns, adverbs and connectives can make pupils' writing more interesting and also help their analysis of text. Explain to pupils that pronouns are used in place of nouns and help make their writing more interesting and varied. Display a short piece of writing such as the following in which no pronouns are used:

> Paul went to town to buy some shoes. Paul saw
> Carol and Paul and Carol went shopping together.
> Carol wanted to buy Paul a birthday present
> but Carol didn't know what Paul wanted. Paul
> and Carol stopped for a coffee and Paul and
> Carol's friend Ian saw Paul and Carol. Ian wanted
> some cake and so Paul bought Ian and Carol a
> slice each.

PRONOUNS

Ask for a volunteer to read the piece aloud, substituting every instance of 'Paul' or 'Carol' with a pronoun from the following displayed list: me, my, I, mine, she, her, hers, he, his, our, we, us, they, them, you, your and it. Pupils should note that by using *only* pronouns the passage becomes equally difficult to understand. The identity of the subject becomes lost and meaning becomes obscured. In pairs, ask pupils to rewrite the passage again, using a mixture of pronouns and proper nouns so that meaning is clear throughout, but excessive repetition is avoided.

ADVERBS

Adverbs can make writing far more effective. While they can give information about *when* (e.g. yesterday) and *where* (e.g. over there) a verb occurs, pupils will be more familiar and comfortable initially with verbs used to describe *how* (e.g. happily) a verb is undertaken. Prepare strips of paper in two colours. One set is to have verbs written on them and the other, adverbs. Place each set in separate containers and call willing pupils out in turn to pick out one verb and one adverb from the containers. Pupils then act out the combined phrase without mentioning either word, and the rest of the class guess what is being acted out. Combinations may be as relatively straightforward as 'skip happily' or as unusual as 'fish loudly'.

To consolidate the notion of 'how' and to introduce the 'where' and 'when' aspects of adverb use, a similar exercise can be used. Pupils are given a number of verb phrases – as a written or verbal task – and have to add an adverb which addresses how, when and where:

I play football enthusiastically. (How)
I play football outside. (Where)
I play football tomorrow. (When)

This can be reinforced through written tasks such as pupils filling in adverb gaps in a passage prepared by you.

An understanding of a variety of connectives or conjunctions can help pupils move away from stilted, single-clause sentencing and make their writing more interesting and sophisticated. It can also move pupils away from over-reliance on 'and', which can only be a bonus for both pupil and teacher. Pupils are not always familiar with the range of connectives, nor with the relationship between the two joined elements which is suggested by choice of connective. Display sentences such as the following:

CONNECTIVES

> Pat went to town and it was raining.
> Pat went to town because it was raining.
> Pat went to town although it was raining.

Ask pupils to work out how the different connectives have altered the meaning of the sentence and which makes most sense to them. Give pupils three sentences, such as those below, to complete using the connective which they feel fits best:

> I have to stay in _____ my aunt is visiting.
> Our food was horrible _____ we had a nice time anyway.
> Andrew was happy _____ Jim came along and ruined it.

Pupils can then write two sentences with a missing connective and pass them to the pupils next to them to complete. To reinforce this, pupils can then write five sentences describing their day using a different connective in each one.

Again, pupils should be familiar with verbs from KS2. Nonetheless, some revision may be necessary along with some further work looking at verb choice and vocabulary. Remind pupils that verbs are 'doing' words, that is they tell us about what someone or something is doing; and that some are plain to see, such as jumping or laughing, while others are not, such as thinking or remembering.

Ask pupils to write down how many verbs they 'did' yesterday. Many will be common to the class, such as talking or eating along with some others you would probably be advised to guide pupils away from!

Write a selection on the board, interactive whiteboard (IWB) or overhead projector (OHP) and pick one as a category heading. Write this on the board and, as a whole-class task, ask pupils to come up with as many alternative or related words as they can: e.g. Eating – chewing, stuffing, swallowing, gnawing, gobbling, nibbling, etc. Ask pupils if the words have different connotations of what is suggested by each verb.

Once this has been completed, select three more verbs for which pupils can create 'word banks' and ask them to choose one of their own. Pupils can feed back to the class and a class word bank can be created. Pupils then select verbs from the word bank to complete sentences such as:

Lucy _____ to school.

Each sentence is to be written twice, using verbs with different connotations. The task aims to encourage pupils to think about verb choice both in their own writing and that of others. Rather than simply identifying what a verb *is*, it focuses instead on what it *does*. It can be extended by, for example, selecting situations, characters or effects and asking pupils to select an appropriate verb. With some pupils, you may then focus on the inappropriate or unexpected verb, and ask them to discuss the effect this may create.

The comma, like its flying friend the apostrophe, is frequently seen scattered randomly over the page or not seen at all. Pupils need to grasp how the comma affects meaning if they are to use it with understanding. Write/display two sentences such as the following, writing the commas in a different colour to the text:

> The boys who were cold and tired were sent back –
> only the cold and tired boys were sent back.
> The boys, <u>who were cold and tired</u>, were sent back –
> all of the boys were cold and tired and were sent
> back.

Any sentence can be used; the important aspect is that the comma must change meaning. Explain to pupils that the underlined part of the sentence is extra information and so is separated from the main part of the sentence by commas. Give the class further examples to punctuate, such as:

> Lisa who had always been fond of Greg was shocked
> by his behaviour.
> The house usually so clean was now a pig sty.

At least in the first instance, ask the whole class to identify the 'extra information' that will need to go in commas. The sentence should make complete sense without the extra information. Once agreed, it can be underlined.

Pupils need then to look at how commas can be used to separate items on a list. Show them a sentence such as the following:

> She went to buy pasta bread oranges cat food sugar
> and cheese.

Ask a volunteer to add commas to the list and then ask pupils to write their own lists which are to be punctuated by their partner. This can be extended to include, for example, compound sentences that consist of two clauses separated by a comma. These can be examined or whole passages can be given to the class to punctuate. Consistently accurate comma use will be very difficult for many, but with repetition of tasks such as these, pupils' accuracy can only improve.

WHERE DO COMMAS GO?

WHAT'S AN APOSTROPHE?

The apostrophe can cause all sorts of problems. Some pupils see them as a decorative flourish that adorns most words ending in 's', while some will steer well clear of them for fear of being wrong. There are fairly straightforward rules which apply to apostrophe use which will need to be taught explicitly if they are to really stick. The following definitions and exercises are a base upon which further tasks can be built.

The apostrophe has two main uses. The first is covered here and the second in Idea 13. The first is: to indicate missing letters. This is seen when two words are joined together to make one. For example:

> I am becomes I'm.
> He is becomes he's.
> Did not becomes didn't.

The place where the missing letter would be is replaced with an apostrophe, to indicate where the letter was taken from. This makes meaning clearer and helps us to avoid confusing words such as 'were' with 'we're'.

Ask your class to rewrite the following sentences using an apostrophe to show how you have shortened the words underlined:

> Julie is not going to the beach.
> I cannot see the stage.
> The floor was not very clean.

Now try to do the reverse. Ask them to write the following out in full, replacing the apostrophe with the missing letters:

> He's a good footballer.
> Natalie hadn't been to Greece before.
> It's a long time until my next holiday.

It is usually the second type of apostrophe use which causes the most confusion, and pupils need to be taught explicitly where to place the apostrophe rather than just the rule. Ask pupils to write the rule and explanation down, but most importantly, get them *using* it. The following suggested rule and tasks can be adapted or extended depending on your class.

The second use of the apostrophe is: to indicate when something belongs to someone or something. This is seen when an apostrophe is put in immediately after the owner. An 's' is added too, e.g. Kate's bag. If the owner ends in an s, you do not always add 's if it is not voiced. For example. 'the boys' room'. You do not pronounce an 's' after boys, so there is no 's' added. Usually, you add the 's' wherever it is pronounced, e.g. Chris's ball. But this is the cause of some debate and it depends on your own style. As long as you are consistent, you will not confuse your pupils!

A simple way to remember when to put in an apostrophe is to ask the question: *To whom or what does it belong?* Put the apostrophe in immediately after the answer. For example:

Item	To whom or what does it belong?	Apostrophe inserted
The chefs hat	The chef★	The chef's hat
Chris hair	Chris★	Chris's hair
The boys changing rooms (more than one boy)	The boys★	The boys' changing rooms
The girls bag (one girl)	The girl★	The girl's bag

Once this has been copied, ask the class questions to check understanding and then ask them to complete a table such as the following:

Sentence	To whom or what does it belong?	With an apostrophe
The howl of the dog was pitiful.	The dog*	
The face of the mountain was treacherous.	The mountain*	

Pupils can then write five apostrophe-free sentences of their own and pass them to their partner to punctuate. The pairs can then check their answers against the rules.

The use of direct speech in a piece of text, when executed well, has many merits: characters can develop their own voices; pupils can show understanding of more complex, internal punctuation (often a way to raise a level) and writing is injected with more variety. Unfortunately, writing direct speech accurately can cause pupils significant problems: speech marks may be used, but in the wrong place; capitalization is often forgotten and internal punctuation can be a mystery. It seems to be that because there are a few rules attached to the writing of speech, many pupils become confused and apply them inconsistently.

One of the most common and easily remedied problems lies in deciding where to put speech marks. Pupils often place them around every word connected to speech indiscriminately. For example, 'Simon said I am not going to school and you can't make me.'

A quick and effective way to rectify this is to write a number of unpunctuated sentences containing direct speech on the board. Depending on the needs of your class these can be graduated in terms of difficulty. Read out the parts of the sentence that are not direct speech and get pupil volunteers to read out what is actually said. This can then be underlined both on the board and in pupils' books. For example:

Simon said <u>why should I go to school</u>
<u>Well then</u> replied Jo <u>please yourself</u>

Pupils can then, of course, put speech marks in place, using the underlining as a guide. This very simple method seems to be effective for many pupils, appealing to visual, aural and kinaesthetic learners.

CAPITAL LETTERS AND
PUNCTUATION IN SPEECH

The next stage is ensuring capitalization is accurate. This does seem to be a very confusing rule at first glance. Pupils are taught throughout school that a sentence starts with a capital letter and then they are told to start speech with one too, even if it starts in the middle of a sentence. It is, however, a relatively straightforward rule to remember. Continue the exercise from the previous idea asking pupils to *start* speech with a capital letter, no matter where it occurs in a sentence.

Simon said 'Why should I go to school'
'Well then' replied Jo 'please yourself'

Punctuation is the next step and one that many find quite hard to grasp. To keep it simple, as a first stage ensure that pupils remember to place a punctuation mark – question mark, full stop, comma or exclamation mark – at the end of speech inside the speech marks. Use a number of simple examples such as those below and allow pupils to select which punctuation mark they think fits best.

'What's for tea' asked Julie.
Matthew shouted 'I won't play then'

The next stage is to separate the spoken word from the speech tag by punctuation – usually a comma. Again, provide a number of examples for pupils to punctuate. Remember to inform pupils that a comma is not needed if speech ends with an exclamation mark, full stop or question mark and comes after the speech tag. A comma is, therefore, always needed when the speech tag comes at the start of the sentence.

> Simon said, 'Why should I go to school?'
> 'Well then,' replied Jo, 'please yourself.'
> 'Where is the canteen?' asked Ishmael.

The final rule for pupils to use is to start a new line for a new speaker, remembering to put the whole sentence on a new line, not simply the spoken words. To ensure retention of these rules it is useful to ensure that they have been used step by step to build up to well-punctuated sentences and that pupils have them written down in their books and refer to them frequently. Regular, short punctuation tasks can be used as effective lesson starters or homework exercises.

Once these rules have been established, encourage pupils to develop their writing by, for example, selecting interesting verbs for speech rather than simply relying on 'said'. Perhaps create a class word bank of alternative words such as 'screamed', 'suggested', 'yelled', 'sobbed', 'hissed' and so on. Cloze exercises using the word bank can be developed showing how selecting more interesting verbs for speech can create more sophisticated and effective writing. Ask pupils to consider the different impressions created by the following and then ask them to use the word banks to create their own variations on sentences you have provided.

> Simon whispered, 'Why should I go to school?'
> Simon screamed, 'Why should I go to school?'

HOW DO YOU SPELL . . . ?
SOME TROUBLESOME WORDS

While some spelling errors are quite unfathomable, there are certain words which come up time and time again. Here is a list of ten of the most common: separate, independent, friend, library, immediately, beginning, sincerely, amount, definitely, occasion.

You are no doubt familiar with these and other usual suspects already! Use this list, or devise one pertinent to the needs of your class, as a spelling test or vocabulary exercise. Ask pupils to keep a spelling diary, at the back of their books maybe, where spelling corrections and troublesome words can be kept.

Other than specific words, common spelling patterns or rules can cause spelling to go awry. Give pupils the following rules to copy and test them on each section. The following tasks and exercises help to clarify some of the most frequently misunderstood.

THE DISAPPEARING 'E'

Why does 'confuse' become 'confusing' but 'care' become 'careful'? Generally, if a *suffix* (letters added to the end of a word to change its meaning) begins with a *consonant* and is added to a word which ends with an 'e', the 'e' will be kept and the suffix added on. For example:

engage + ment = engagement
hope + less = hopeless
secure + ly = securely.

If, on the other hand, the suffix starts with a *vowel*, it is usually the case that the 'e' will be removed before the suffix is added. For example:

believe + able = believable
investigate + ion = investigation
move + ing = moving.

SWIMMING OR SWIMING

Why do some words have a double letter added in the middle? Usually, if a word has *one syllable* and ends with *one consonant*, the last consonant will be *doubled*. For example:

skip = one syllable and one consonant at end = skipping
jump = one syllable and two consonants at end = jumping
hit = one syllable and one consonant at end = hitting

I CAN SEE CLEARLY NOW –
TIPS FOR IMPROVING HANDWRITING

For many pupils, word-processing has been a real boon. Not only can their spelling and grammar be checked – to quite unusual results at times – but their words can be seen clearly and unambiguously. While this is, on the whole, a real benefit, it does not do away with the need for pupils to be able to write legibly, both in class and in examinations. While many individuals will find it almost impossible to develop textbook handwriting – particularly during the hurried environment of the examination room – it is possible to provide pupils with some tips and exercises which will go some way to making their writing much more easy to decipher. Many pupils rush their writing and Ideas 19 and 20, while a little rudimentary and old-fashioned, are aimed at encouraging control.

Firstly, make sure that pupils are sitting up, with both feet on the floor and leaning forward a little but without their heads near the paper. The paper should be in line with the shoulder of the hand with which they write, rather than in the middle. Pens should be held by the thumb and forefinger, with the middle finger giving further support, but this can vary to a degree according to what feels most comfortable.

Ask pupils to practise grip and pen hold by moving the pen up and down the page in diagonal and vertical strokes, such as the following:

Try to ensure that the pen strokes are as regular as possible and pupils are controlling their pens rather than just scribbling on the page. Similarly, ask them to draw some controlled circles and waves, paying attention to size and consistency. While this may seem a little lacking in focus, these exercises can help pupils develop a 'motor' memory. Think about how you sometimes need to write a word to check its spelling – that is your motor memory at work. Teaching pupils 'joined up' writing can help with their spelling, as patterns are learned and remembered even if a child may not know a spelling when asked.

POSITION AND PEN CONTROL

Next, move them on to letters. Remember to focus not on notions of 'correctness' as such, as handwriting is very individual, but rather on clarity.

Many pupils do not form their letters completely. Focus pupils' attention on the difference in size and relationship to the line between, for example, 'd', 'a' and 'j'. This needs to be emphasized, particularly as many pupils (often girls for some reason) write each letter the same height and width, resulting in a difficult-to-read 'fat bubble' effect. Ask them to write the alphabet quickly, not joined at this point, ensuring that each letter is properly formed. Letters with 'tails' should be roughly twice the size of those without, as are capital letters. For some pupils, this sort of clarity will be improvement enough, but for others press on with tasks which encourage appropriate joining of letters.

Show pupils the alphabet, on OHP, board or IWB, fully joined up. Point out diagonal joins, horizontal joins and those letters that do not join. You may also want to point out that a, c, d, e, h, i, k, l, m, n, t, and u join to e, i, j, m, n, p, r, u, v, w, x and y but not to a, c, d, g, o, q, s, b, d, f, h, k, l or t. Or you may think that is a complication too far at this stage! Keeping the alphabet on display, ask pupils to write a selection of words that are joined in a variety of ways, such as: college, date, spoon, twist, should, jump, teach, week and jam.

Having already checked pupils' work during the exercise, select pupils to come to the front of the class and share what they have done. Extend the task by giving further words to write or a short paragraph. The time spent on each element and the degree of guidance provided will depend very much on the needs of the class or pupil. Do try to reinforce the skills developed here, perhaps by having a handwriting exercise as a lesson starter and by praising those whose handwriting improves the most. This is one area where practice really does make all the difference.

Writing

As English teachers, we often spend the bulk of our time focused firmly on the written word. While this is understandable, pictures have an important role to play in the English classroom. Most examination boards use pictures in some form. This will often be in those sections where pupils analyse or comment upon images used in non-fiction texts such as advertisements or newspapers. Others have used an image as a kick-start to a piece of descriptive writing, for example. By using images in our classrooms, we may reach those pupils who may find text difficult to access. We also give opportunities for pupils to explore meaning on their own terms and in their own way. Many pupils, when faced with the written word, feel that they have to decode and decipher and then find THE answer. A great many may feel that they cannot do this and that they, therefore, can't 'do' English.

Pictures can be used to great effect in the classroom as a way of exploring an idea or character; initiating questions; summing up or recapping; exploring connections and emotions – the possibilities are considerable. Collect any interesting images you find and laminate if possible. Try to make your collection as varied as possible and use a variety of sources.

Below are some suggestions for using the pictures you have collected (see Idea 21):

○ Lay out a selection of pictures and ask pupils to select the one they feel most represents a given character or aspect of that character. They then have to explain their choice. For example, one pupil in a class of mine chose a picture of a derelict block of flats to represent Macbeth as he felt that they both once had great promise, but were now nasty reminders of what should have been.

○ Similarly, pupils can select a picture they feel best represents how a character may be feeling at a given time. Again, encourage your pupils to explain their choices. It is through their explanations that they begin to explore meaning and, often, unencumbered by text, many pupils find they are able to explain their choices in quite sophisticated ways.

○ Pictures can be used, of course as stimulus for discussion and debate. Pupils can select or bring in pictures of their own that they think sum up a particular point of view – an animal in a cage perhaps, or a landfill. This can then be explored as a whole class with teacher guidance.

○ Read a short story which pupils then retell using a series of, say, five selected images. This can be a useful way of seeing what points of the story they feel are most important and also how they interpret the story. It can lead to quite varied responses, which can in turn lead to interesting discussions.

○ Ask pupils to select an image they feel most striking or about which they want to learn more. They can then go into groups of three and agree on the picture that has raised the most interesting questions. Try to guide pupils away from questions *about* the image as such and towards questions *raised* by the image. For example, a picture of an empty room may begin a discussion on loneliness – carefully facilitated by you. This approach owes a lot to Philosophy for Children – something that could play a very important role in our classrooms.

It is sometimes thought that the 'story' is the form of writing most easily accessible to pupils. After all, they have been writing them for most of their school lives and are familiar with the form. However, the writing of a good story is not necessarily an innate gift and some of the basic mechanics can be taught so as to improve the story-writing skills of all pupils. Many of the tasks in other sections, such as Idea 39 'Who? Understanding character', and Idea 4 'Adjectives' can also be used to inform pupils' own writing. The following are additional ideas that can be used to focus pupils on features of a good story and encourage them to improve their own writing

Put the class into groups and distribute three (very) short stories to each. Ask pupils to put the stories in rank order and to write a brief explanation for their decision. Introduce pupils to the basic planning format of:

○ opening;
○ plot/character development;
○ problem;
○ conclusion/resolution.

Read through one of the extracts with them, indicating how the story would fit this format. Pupils can then write the plan for their favourite of the three extracts using this format. You can use pupils' knowledge of, for example, film or urban myth to reinforce this planning format. Give pupils a genre, such as the spooky story, and ask them to write a plan for their own story using the format.

Next, distribute the opening paragraphs from three stories – each of which should be effective in a different way. Ask pupils to identify – individually or in pairs – key features such as: narrative voice used; any words or phrases that hint at what is to come; a detailed description of a place, person or object; opening sentence; any characters or situations that are introduced; what action occurs. If possible, pupils can comment on what effect any of these features helps create. Pupils can feed back to the class and share ideas. From the feedback, produce a list of effective elements.

Ask pupils to choose which opening they find most effective and use this to model the opening to their own story. If time allows, volunteers can read their story openings and pupils can raise their hand each time a particular effect is noticed and explain what they have spotted.

Read through three descriptions of characters with the class. Ask the class to note how we learn about each character and a class spider diagram can be made on the board from their observations, including points such as: how a character looks; what they say and how they speak; how other characters react to them; any imagery used to describe them and so on. Distribute to pairs of pupils cards that identify two characters; their relationship; basic characteristics and, most importantly, how you want readers to react towards the characters. Each pair can then write a paragraph that sets the characters up for the reader. Select paragraphs to be read aloud and ask pupils to note down how they feel about the characters, and why they feel that way. After the reading, pupils can share their observations.

Pupils need to inject detail and atmosphere into their stories. Draw the outline of a body on the board. (An IWB is perfect for this if you are lucky enough to have one.) Ask pupils to do the same in their books, leaving plenty of room around their drawing for labelling. Initiate a brief discussion about how the body reacts when scared – for example, hair stands on end, shivers run up the spine and so on. Label the body on the board with one example and explain that they will be given 5–10 minutes to label their drawings with as many reactions as they can. While pupils are engaged in this, it is useful to monitor their responses and pick up on any particularly interesting examples you may wish to call on later – as well as those you may want to avoid!

Once their time is up, invite pupils up to the board to label the drawing with one of their examples. When you feel the labelling on the board is detailed enough, ask pupils to copy down any suggestions they may have missed, so that each pupil has a complete set of reactions labelled on their drawing. This can, of course, be adapted to fit other emotions, such as love. Pupils can then write five short sentences featuring their observations.

This is a follow-up task to the 'map of the body' seen in Idea 25. It can also be adapted to fit many types of story or can be used as a stand-alone task. The focus this time is setting. Draw the outline of a house on the board and ask pupils to think about elements that could create a scary atmosphere. Discussion may be initiated by asking pupils to think about what scares them when they are alone in the house. Label the drawing with one example, such as creaking floorboards, or the eyes of a painting that seems to follow you. Again, pupils have between 5 to 10 minutes to label their own drawings and then feed back to the class. Once sufficient ideas have been collected, pupils can copy any suggestions they missed.

The two tasks are then brought together. Pupils are to write five compound or complex sentences using the information found in their drawings. Write down two features from the drawing of the body and two from that of the house, then ask pupils to connect them to make two sentences, such as:

> The trees brushed against the windows and the hairs on the back of her neck stood on end.
> As the door creaked open a shiver ran down my spine.

Be sure to use pupils' knowledge from other lessons to inform their writing. Effective dialogue; variety in sentence structure; thoughtful selection of verbs, adverbs and adjectives; narrative voice and use of alliteration, metaphor and simile can all help to make stories more effective.

Pupils use metaphor and simile quite frequently, although they may not recognize it as such. Phrases such as 'you pig', 'I am boiling', 'stop acting like a baby', 'pizza face' and so on are regular features of the soundscape of a school. While pupils may use metaphor and simile with relative impunity, they need to understand how they are identified, how they work and how to use this understanding effectively in their own reading and writing.

Give pupils a definition for both metaphor and simile, emphasizing that metaphor describes one thing *as if it is another* and simile uses the words *as* or *like*. Pupils need to write the definition in their books, along with an example of each. Next, distribute a list of metaphors and similes. Pupils have to correctly identify each sentence. Class share responses and any anomalies or difficulties are discussed.

Select a few common examples of metaphors and similes and display them to the class. Ask the class to write down what each suggests, as well as the literal meaning such as:

'You pig' means someone is dirty or greedy
    (metaphor).
'You pig' means something is a pink farmyard animal
    with a curly tail (literal).

LITERAL VERSUS METAPHORICAL

The class should note that metaphorical use is very different from literal. Metaphors and similes generally compare two things that are different in most ways except for one. Direct pupil attention back to the examples of similes and metaphors and ask them to write alongside each example what element is being identified as similar. For example: 'You pig' compares the way someone eats to that of a pig. Ask pupils to select the most likely comparison from examples such as the following:

That test was rock hard:
a) It was made of a solid substance, like rock.
b) It was difficult to get through.
c) It was sweet tasting.

My love is like the sun:
a) She is big, round and yellow.
b) She is gaseous.
c) She is the centre of everything for me.

The sophistication of the examples used can vary as can the level of support given. The main aim is to encourage pupils to think about what is being suggested by a metaphor or a simile. They can also use this format to write about metaphor and simile. For example, 'The simile "my love is like the sun" suggests that she is the centre of the writer's universe.'

Display some sentence starters and ask pupils to complete them using metaphor or simile. For example:

Peter sprinted down the pitch like . . .
Your hair is . . .
Her skin felt like . . .
The dancers are . . .

Depending on the needs of your class, you may guide them towards metaphors that do not use 'is' as a marker, such as:

My mind raced through the possible answers.

He appeared, an angry bull ready to knock down
anything in his way.

Pupils can underline any words that are used
metaphorically and describe what effect the metaphor has.

FORMAL OR INFORMAL?

One of the easiest ways to introduce the idea of informal and formal language is by way of the letter. Pupils should be aware of the layout of a formal letter. Prepare a model pair of letters that are based on the same basic subject, and distribute copies or present on an IWB or OHP. Ask pupils to write down the audience and purpose of each letter. For example, Letter A is for a friend and is describing a holiday and Letter B is for a customer and is selling a holiday. In a table, pupils then write down five features (as far as possible) from each letter that made them come to their conclusion regarding audience and purpose. This can include features such as layout, greeting, vocabulary and so on.

Feedback from this task is then used to produce a short and clear set of class rules for formal and informal letters, which are recorded in pupils' books. Distribute to each pupil a slip of paper with an audience, e.g. 'grandparent', and purpose, e.g. 'Thanking them for the horrible jumper they gave you (again) for your birthday'; or 'Local newspaper' and 'Complaining about the mess in a local park'. Pupils then write a short letter using this and the rules as their guideline.

After a short while (try not to run the letter writing too long at this stage), pupils swap letters and decide what they think the intended audience and purpose are and to think of three reasons for their choices. Feed back from a selection to check rules are understood.

As homework or further task, ask pupils to write an informal and a formal letter about the same topic, but to different audiences. For example, complaining about a neighbour's noise to your sister and to the police; a holiday postcard to a friend and your boss; or the 'interests' section of a job application and an advert for a pen pal.

This stage lends itself to some of the speaking and listening tasks in Section 8. Ask pupils to produce a talk for a given pair of audiences about the same topic. This can also be a good time to remind them of the information that body language can provide and tone of voice. As a piece of self-assessment, ask pupils to give five reasons for choices they made in their speeches and to judge which they thought most and least effective and why.

This type of writing is often more difficult than it seems. Pupils tend towards writing narrative rather than description and so this needs special focus. Prior to descriptive writing tasks, pupils should be made more familiar with word level exercises such as those for adjective and adverb selection.

Ask pupils to write the five senses in their books, leaving around five lines underneath each. Once this is complete, ask pupils to imagine they are in a familiar environment, such as the school canteen, and to think of what they see, hear, smell, taste and touch. Reinforce the idea of paying close attention to everything they can think of. For example, rather than the door being simply white, is it freshly painted? Graffiti-covered? Chipped and cracked? Most of the description offered will be of things seen or heard, but emphasize the need to create as complete a picture as possible using the other senses too. Complete a class spider diagram with all of their observations. These will include things like the smell of vinegar and children shouting. Pupils then write each of the observations under the appropriate sense in their books.

Next, ask pupils to write a short description of a familiar place or thing using as many of their senses as they can, but without naming what it is they are describing. Volunteers can read their work to the class who then guess what is being described. For example, 'Yet again it is packed full of people, jostling for just one of the rows of cloth and metal seats. People are squashed; standing pressed so close together that they can smell each other's breath. It moves and some lose their balance, shopping spilling out from bags balanced between knees.'

To continue the task, pupils can write about their own rooms, for example. If suitable, these can be swapped and pupils can draw one another's rooms based on the description given. The drawings can then be given back to the pupil whose room it is, to see if it is accurate. Any discrepancies can be discussed with the description as the basis. Further tasks can also be set which establish the notion of static or travelling viewpoint.

WRITING TO PERSUADE

Pupils are familiar with these types of text and the language they use in their everyday lives. Advertisements bombard them from every angle and many pupils are themselves quite skilled in the art of persuasion! Many do, however, find it surprisingly difficult to work out explicitly *how* these types of text work. It is therefore often best to pick a few specific and familiar features of persuasive text and focus on these rather than risk muddying the waters with an exhausting list of examples. This enables you to focus the lesson(s) on technique and device rather than simply spotting different text types.

Distribute, in whichever way suits you and your class best, a glossary of persuasive devices such as: the rhetorical question; rule of three; 'stick and carrot'; hyperbole; repetition; use of emotive language, and flattery, etc.

Ask pupils to role-play in pairs the following scenario. A teenager is desperate to go to a birthday party at a friend's house. Their parent is adamant that, following the teenager's late arrival home after the last party, they will not be allowed to go. The teenager's task is to persuade the parent to change their mind, using as many techniques as they can. Many may find it surprisingly difficult to sustain an argument for very long. Ensure that pupils are familiar with devices so that they can be used to frame their attempts at persuasion. Monitor the exercise and select good examples to show to the rest of the class, asking the class to tick off any persuasive techniques they spot.

Autobiographical writing has several positive elements, perhaps the most important of which is the fact that pupils are given the opportunity to write about an area in which they are the expert. It can be a rewarding task that can be accessed by pupils of different abilities, and can utilize a variety of skills and tasks. The following suggestions can be used in any order you feel most suitable for your class.

Explain what autobiography is (most pupils will have some idea of this). Give the class extracts from autobiographical works and read through. The texts should reflect a wide range of styles and subjects. Ask the class to identify key features of autobiographical writing. These should include the use of the first person; exploration of thoughts and feelings; one-sided perspective; selection and editing and so on, and can be made into a set of guidelines that can be displayed throughout the series of lessons.

Remind pupils that autobiographical works do not tell every detail of a life but rather select key elements. Ask the class to think of a memorable story from their time at junior school. Pupils need to consider why this is an important memory for them. Is it humorous, sad, tense? Did it change them in any way? Did they learn something from it? Did it change others' opinions of them? Pupils can then share their stories in pairs. This can be repeated to include memorable holidays, parties or school trips, for example. There may be a degree of sensitivity required in some instances as pupils' circumstances and experiences may vary greatly.

ALL ABOUT ME – WHAT IS AUTOBIOGRAPHY?

ME, ME, ME – WRITING AUTOBIOGRAPHY

Pupils can complete a timeline of their lives so far, indicating a key memory for each year. This can be used as a planning tool for their own autobiographical writing. Pupils can also keep an image diary of key places and people. This may include sketches of their old school, friends or family members; photos; detailed descriptions of bedrooms or favourite toys and so on. Ask pupils to bring in to class an object that holds strong memories for them. (Be sure that parents are informed.) It may be a photograph, a favourite toy, a gift from a grandparent, a holiday memento . . . the list is endless. Pupils can then explain to the class the reasons why that object is so important to them. Pupils can also create a coat of arms for themselves using those things they feel represent them. These can then be used as display work.

Give pupils a plan to use for framing their own autobiographies. This helps their writing have more scope and variety and also organizes the task into manageable chunks. Some suggested sections may be earliest memories; first day at school; memories of junior school; my family; proudest day; my future and so on. If possible and appropriate, encourage pupils to research their family stories.

Familiarize pupils with the format of a book. Pay attention to features such as cover, title, blurb and publishing details. Pupils can then present their own autobiographies in book form, complete with reviews and author information.

Shared writing can be a great tool for exploring texts. We often shy away from this sort of activity in secondary school – perhaps because we may feel it is difficult to assess. This is a shame. Pupils who may feel insecure as writers can really benefit from this sort of modelling and those who are more confident get an opportunity to think explicitly about what they may do intuitively.

Organize the pupils into groups of four or five. Agree as a class the kind of story you will write and then set each group the task of creating characters (or a character) for the story. Each group then feeds back, outlining their character and explaining why they would be good for the story. The class then agree, with your guidance, on which characters they are going to use.

The class can then work on the opening of their story. Pupils suggest sentences which are then modified by the class. Adjectives can be added, punctuation altered, action dropped in or removed. Be sure to direct focus onto the impact that certain words or phrases have. This sort of session works best if you have access to a data projector so that text can be edited easily and visibly. It is important that pupils can see the editing and drafting process as it occurs.

Aim to get as many different contributions as you can. The collaborative group nature of the writing needs to be reinforced.

You can, of course opt to write an opening paragraph in this whole-class fashion and then ask pupils to complete the rest of the story individually or in their groups, using what they have learned from the collaborative exercise.

COLLABORATIVE WRITING

There any many other tasks and ideas that can be used when pupils are writing autobiographical pieces. These types of tasks can be very rewarding in a number of ways. For example, they allow the class to find out more about each other; they encourage pupils to reflect and consider those events, people and things that are most significant to them and why; and pupils of all abilities will be able to participate at some level, as the subject is known to them, and pupils can explore a variety of text types and utilize a range of skills. The following are suggestions that can extend and develop work on pupils' own autobiographical writing.

Ask pupils to bring in (if possible) a copy of their first favourite song or songs that remind them of specific events such as their first school disco, a holiday or Christmas. Music can be incredibly evocative and pupils often find that their memories are awoken by one another's choices. In a similar vein, a more Proustian take on the same task can be very effective, due to the famously evocative nature of the sense of smell. In sealed jars, bring in evocative smells such as some fresh grass, baby powder, vinegar, pine needles or generic bubble bath. Ask blindfolded pupils to smell a selected jar and then to describe to the class any memories that the smell may evoke. You can organize this in the way you feel most suitable.

Pupils can interview one another using pre-prepared questions. These can be then presented in either written form as a magazine Q&A, for example, or as a television/radio interview. Pupils can also produce a print, radio or television advert for their autobiographies, selecting those elements they think will attract a readership and presenting them accordingly.

Pupils can use their drama skills to present aspects of their life stories in a number of ways. Tableau and thought tracking can be used to considerable effect. Pupils can script key scenes from their lives and perform them in groups – the author acting as director. See Section 10 Drama in the English classroom for more details.

Introducing reading and understanding

DEVELOPING DEDUCTION

As English teachers, we encourage our pupils to read for clues and to be able to infer, deduce and understand connotation. Tasks such as these enhance our pupils' reading, writing and thinking skills. The following task and its variants are best organized as group or paired activities, as discussion and debate are important aspects in terms of outcome and process. You can choose to use these activities over several lessons. The number of lessons needed will depend on your intended outcome and the needs of the class.

Prepare an image of a flat or house. You can use collage, ICT, sketching or any other method most suitable for you, although an IWB is by far the most useful here. Display or distribute the image to the class. Tell them that the property has been found empty and that, as investigators, they have to find out as much as possible about the occupant and where they may have gone. Be sure to provide sufficient detail for the pupils – torn curtains, pristine hedges, ornate door furniture, bars over the windows or a child's toy hanging up, for example. Ask pupils to note down their thoughts about the occupants. They can then feed back to class, giving reasons for their deductions. Next, display or distribute a picture or series of pictures of the interior of the property. Again, provide potential clues in your images – a torn calendar, a space where a picture might have been, bookcases filled with carefully selected texts, a home gym, photographs, car keys on a bedside table and so on. Ask pupils to develop their investigation in the light of their new findings and report back to the class with their deductions regarding the occupants and where they may now be. A number of tasks can be set at this point – you may choose to ask your pupils to draw character profiles of the occupant/s and use these, alongside their deductions, to write a narrative leading up to the point at which the property was vacated; a report about their findings; a series of questions to ask other groups so as to come to an agreed set of events or a newspaper story, among other options. You can, of course, differentiate this task fairly easily simply by varying the types and number of clues you leave.

The following ideas can be used to supplement the previous idea or as stand-alone tasks.

You could bring into class a ready-prepared bag of shopping which has been found in a specific location – for example, on a bus, at an ice-skating rink, in a nightclub or in a phone box. Explain to pupils that they have been charged, as investigators, with painting as full a picture as possible of the person who has left this bag behind, based on its contents and the location in which it was found.

Similarly, present to the class several items that have been found in a bin or in a car. Include items such as receipts, hair clips, CDs, torn envelopes, travel tickets and so on.

These tasks can be combined to make an extended activity over a series of lessons with further additions from you – a tape recording of a phone message, or an item of clothing, for example. There are a number of possible end tasks that can be undertaken once pupils have completed their investigations. They may be asked to present their findings to the class as a speaking and listening assessment; to write up their accounts as a formal report, to write a narrative or a play script, to produce a news programme or newspaper story – amongst many other possibilities.

MORE DEDUCTION

CLOSE READING OF PERSUASIVE TEXT

Distribute a piece of persuasive writing and have a copy which can be displayed to the whole class on an OHP, IWB, or a very large photocopy attached to the board. Often, it is most effective to produce a text of your own which contains as many devices as are appropriate for your class, but if that isn't possible, select one which is appropriately pitched as very sophisticated persuasive pieces are often too subtle for many pupils to appreciate. Try not to make the text too long – sustained focus is required here to identify the features that make the piece work. Read through the piece and ask pupils to identify persuasive techniques in pairs or individually. Pupils are then selected in turn to annotate the whole-class copy of the text. Any features which pupils missed can then be noted on their own copy. Using this text as a model, pupils then produce their own persuasive piece of writing on a topic selected or agreed upon by you for suitability.

Other tasks can of course be added to this basic framework at any stage. For example, individual features can be highlighted by sentence starters for 'rule of three' or 'stick and carrot' for pupils to complete; vocabulary and phrase banks can be provided as a writing frame; the introduction to persuasive writing can be extended by looking at a variety of persuasive texts, or the glossary can be used as a task focus, with pupils asked to provide an example for each feature.

A thorough understanding of character is the key into narrative texts for many pupils. It is also a good way to begin teaching close analysis of text, lending itself as it does to close reading and inference. We can find out about a character in many ways – for example, what they do and how; the way they look; what they say and how others react to them. The following exercises encourage pupils to explore why they react to certain characters in particular ways.

Have pupils read the following passages and then answer the questions underneath.

> Steven shuffled into the classroom, his gaze fixed firmly on his grubby, unfashionable trainers.
> He had always been small for his age – quiet, too.
> He hadn't just 'grown up and out of it' as his mum had promised him so many times.
>
> 'Maybe if I stay just here, they won't notice me,' he thought to himself.
>
> There was to be no such luck.
>
> 'Nice shoes, Mouseboy! Look at them. What a state!'
>
> The whole class turned to look; their laughter turning his face an even deeper shade of red.

❍ How do you think Steven feels about entering his classroom? Which word or words make you think that? What may this tell you about him?
❍ Do you think he has felt this way for a while? What makes you think that? What could this tell us about Steven?
❍ What do you think his classmates think of him? Why do you think that? What may this tell us about Steven?

Fill in the table (overleaf) with three words or phrases to describe Steven. In the second column, write down words from the passage to back up your point.

WHO? UNDERSTANDING CHARACTER

Steven is . . .	I think this because the passage says . . .

The same basic skills are used to understand atmosphere. Through close reading, pupils are encouraged to identify *how* a particular impression is created. While these tasks and skills are used here to aid understanding of text, they also help pupils develop their writing skills by showing them explicitly how writers create certain effects – skills which they can then employ in their own writing. The following tasks help pupils build awareness of how effects are created. Ask pupils to read the following sentence carefully:

Sara <u>skipped</u> through the <u>sun-dappled</u> woods. Birds <u>sang sweetly</u> from the <u>lush, green</u> trees and the ground felt <u>soft</u> beneath her feet.

The picture created here is very sweet and pleasant, almost like a Disney film! Pupils are then to focus on how just a few word changes can change atmosphere:

Sara <u>crept</u> through the <u>storm-struck</u> woods. Birds <u>screeched menacingly</u> from the <u>bare, overgrown</u> trees and the ground felt <u>brittle</u> beneath her feet.

Just by changing a few words, a totally different atmosphere is created. Ask pupils to transform the following sentence:

The school canteen was full of <u>well-behaved children chatting quietly</u> and the <u>sweet smell</u> of <u>delicious food</u>.

See if they can identify what kind of words are changed. Are they nouns? Adjectives? Verbs?

Many different parts of speech can be substituted to create new meaning and atmosphere. The most common tend to be adjectives, verbs and adverbs – all of which are covered in other sections. Tasks can be devised – either as extension or for the whole class – that reinforce this. For example, pupils can make adjective or verb banks of particular atmospheric types or connections can be made as to the connotations of certain words.

WHAT IS ATMOSPHERE?

There is more to atmosphere than word choice alone, and more to analysis than identification and substitution. The following tasks help pupils to look at the part other features play in the creation of atmosphere.

Pupils make associations between seemingly unrelated things in their everyday life. Capitalize on this by asking them to complete a table such as the following:

Emotion	Colour	Animal	Weather	Food
Love	Red	Cat	Hot sun with some storms	A big juicy apple

This can, of course, be extended or altered to cover a range of emotions either pre-selected by you or of the pupils' choice. Discuss some of the selections and ask the class to write reasons for all or a selection of their answers, which are in turn, shared with the class. For example, '*Love* reminds me of a summer storm because it can be sunny and warm one minute and cloudy and stormy the next.' Try to encourage pupils to think about their reasons carefully.

Once pupils have begun to understand that links such as those in Idea 41 can be made, ask them to think for a moment about any films they have seen, which have, for example, a scary atmosphere. Ask them to list some common features in pairs and then feed back to the rest of the class. These may include features such as: thunder and lightning, a deserted building, dark places (setting), a stranger, a monster, an escaped killer, a main hero or heroine who saves the day (character), an ancient secret, hidden riches, revenge (plot), unexpected noises, surprise elements, tense music, close ups and fast camera work (devices) and so on.

Again, select some of these and ask pupils to write down five, with reasons as to why they are elements of a scary atmosphere and how they work to make the viewer afraid. For example, 'A deserted building can be scary because no one can come to help you' or 'Dark places are scary because you cannot see what's coming'. Try to guide pupils to focus on presentational elements rather than simply focusing on gory content, and get them into the habit of using the headings of character, plot, setting and devices as it will help them later.

Other types of film can be discussed as well as or instead of horror, depending on your class, and the task can lead well into any work you wish to do on literary genre.

ATMOSPHERE – THE
PUTTING THE PIECES TOGETHER

Following on from the previous tasks, pupils can then write a scene from a film which creates a scary atmosphere. Many pupils are attracted to and familiar with horror, just ensure that the content is suitable. This can be done very effectively as group work, with each group member allocated a particular role, such as 'costume designer'. Again, ensure that pupils pay attention to how their ideas are presented, rather than focus exclusively on content. Each group can give a presentation, discussing their scene and the decisions they made. If appropriate, the class can ask questions.

Many pupils will be far more familiar with films than books and this knowledge can be used effectively. Pupils may, for example, find the creation of suspense through features such as music a good starting point to a discussion of suspense. Similarly, the fast cutting that goes in a chase scene – often to a dead end – can provide a good starting point for a closer look at sentence structure – the fast cuts becoming short, sharp sentences. Both help create a sense of panic and pace. It is this sort of understanding that you want your pupils to aim for. Pick out some common stylistic elements or devices, such as those above, and discuss with the class how this effect could be created in a book. To help ensure retention, this can be noted in table form:

Film	Book
Fast chase upstairs with camera from one character's perspective.	Writing in the first person with short sentences.

Pupils can then transform their film scenes into text extracts.

Having selected your class reader, it is sometimes difficult to come up with varied and engaging tasks that will enhance pupils' understanding and also develop other skills. While shared reading supported by apt questioning can be an important part of lessons, it can quickly become repetitive. The following suggestions can be adapted to suit many texts and help pupils explore the text in different ways. Apart from the first suggestion, they are not in any particular order, and can be used as and when appropriate.

Before starting the novel, pupils can use the information provided by its cover to predict what the book will be about. Ask pupils to note down their thoughts on what type of story they think it will be; where and when it is set; who the main characters will be; and any ideas about plot they may have. If any particular themes are identified, ask the class for their opinions. This sort of prediction task need not take much time and can be a useful way of introducing key ideas. It also encourages pupils to develop their skills of deduction.

INTRODUCING THE CLASS READER

Below are three tasks for getting your students to explore character.

Following a piece of detailed character description, ask pupils to draw the character, using the description as their guide. Pupils can then write a few sentences exploring how the description made them feel about the character, giving reasons for their opinions. Similarly, pupils can create character fact files that contain a drawing and key information, such as age, family and interests. These can be used in later tasks, such as writing newspaper or police reports. While they may seem a little overused, newspaper and school reports can be effective ways of recording key events and impressions.

Use hot seating as a way of exploring character. Allocate characters to pupils and ask them to prepare to answer questions about a particular incident or theme. This can be organized in a chat-show format with several characters appearing as guests, which will encourage pupils to think about relationships in the novel.

If a particular problem presents itself in the narrative, pupils can write a letter in character to an agony aunt along with a reply offering advice. Remind pupils to write *as* the character, voicing *their* concerns in *their* voice. In a similar vein, a diary entry could be written, or a letter to a friend.

Focus on the first chapter of the novel and look at how genre is established through setting, description, language and character. If no obvious genre is established, look at what atmosphere is suggested by time of day, presentation of characters, description of place and use of dialogue. At an appropriate point, give pupils a photocopied section of text and explain what atmosphere, for example, is created in the piece. Ask pupils to underline any features that help create that atmosphere. You then read the extract out and instruct pupils to put up their hands and say 'atmosphere' when any element they have noted is read out. The pupil has to explain their point, and, if agreed by the class, the point is underlined by all. Once all features have been identified, they can be cut out (by you) and used as the basis for a reading and understanding written task.

At the end of each chapter pupils could write a short prediction for the following chapter. They must use all available knowledge so far in the novel as the basis for their prediction. Ask volunteers to read out their prediction and get them also to state the reasons behind their decision. A discussion can then follow with other pupils giving their opinion about the next chapter. It is useful for pupils to keep a record of predictions they make and to go back to them once they have completed the novel.

Following a description of a place, ask pupils to write the name of the place as a heading and write down any words or phrases that create a particular impression. Pupils then note how that impression is based on their findings. This can be extended by pupils writing an estate agent's advert or a brochure, for example.

Pupils can transform the novel into a film or television series. This task is effective in encouraging pupils to select key elements of plot, as well as dramatic highs and lows, features of character, patterns of imagery and so on. Ask pupils to write an outline of their film, including setting, scenes, etc. If it is to be a television series, ask them to think about where each episode will end. Pupils can cast their film/programme, giving reasons for their selections.

Empathy tasks are a good way for pupils to show that they have really got to grips with a character. It does have to be remembered, however, that this is essentially a reading task and that, to gain the best mark they can, pupils need to show not only an understanding of the part a character plays in a narrative, but also that they can express thoughts and feelings that character may have and (for the top levels) use the voice of that character convincingly.

For all empathy tasks it is vital that pupils understand that they are writing *as* a given character rather than *about* them. This necessitates them writing from that character's point of view rather than simply retelling the story in the first person. Ask pupils to write down key things that must be remembered when writing in character. These should include: using the first person throughout; offering the character's viewpoint on events found in the text and accurate setting, period and relationships. It can be of great benefit to pupils if the empathy task has a specific focus. This could be a point of high drama in the text or a significant event. This allows them to choose which other characters are going to be important to mention and also to focus the response of their character more keenly.

SHOWING UNDERSTANDING OF CHARACTER – EMPATHY TASKS

ESTABLISHING YOUR CHARACTER

Ask pupils to write down a 'fact file' containing at least five key facts about the character. These may include, for example, name, age, marital status and occupation. Next ask them to link the character to at least three other characters in the studied text by the nature of relationship and any important information. E.g.

Nurse $\xrightarrow{\text{Care giver}}$ **Juliet**

Loyal, loving and secretive. Has nursed Juliet since she was a baby. Only wants what is best for Juliet, although this means she is prepared to go behind her employer's back.

This stage can be differentiated by asking pupils to add detail about the type of language, imagery or other features used by the character. For example:

Nurse: She is often distracted and will start one story only to go into another. Her lines are 'bitty', with lots of personal anecdote and lots of punctuation such as exclamation marks and dashes. She sometimes uses inappropriate language.

The amount of detail added at this stage will depend on the pupils involved and how much guidance and support you think they will need. To develop this idea further, see the following idea.

To develop the previous idea further, pick a specific focus and ask pupils to make a spider diagram outlining how the character may feel at this point. To continue with *Romeo and Juliet*, if the focus was, for example, the point where Romeo is banished and Capulet has ordered Juliet to marry Paris, the diagram could be something like this:

Upset for Juliet as she knows how much she loves Romeo.

Protective of Juliet in the face of her father's anger.

Worried in case Capulet finds out that she helped them get together.

NURSE'S FEELINGS

Angry and sad about the death of Tybalt.

Concerned that Juliet makes the 'right' decision and forgets Romeo.

The next stage is to decide what format the piece is to take. It could be a personal letter; an interview; a statement to police; a chapter from an autobiography or a diary entry. What is important is that the pupils are clear what type of text they are writing and are already familiar with the format. Ask pupils to write five lines, in character, about one of the points they made in their spider diagram. Check work and ask some pupils to feed back to the rest of the class. To extend this, now focus on language features (this can be done earlier if

STRUCTURING RESPONSES TO EMPATHY TASKS

59

appropriate). Show pupils a typical piece of dialogue from a character and focus them on the most obvious idiosyncrasies or patterns. Ask them to write a simple instruction or statement in the style of the character using the same images, tone and patterns. Pupils can then share their work.

Once you feel all pupils are clear as to the nature of the task, ask them to complete their piece of writing.

Between
the lines –
comprehension
skills

Pupils will complete numerous comprehension exercises during their time in school, both in class and at each end of Key Stage examination. The tasks which help pupils with their writing, such as adjective use, creating atmosphere and so on, introduce the skills that pupils will need to discuss in their analysis of texts. Remind pupils of these lessons and of how they create effects in their own writing.

Some comprehension questions are 'what' questions, which ask pupils to retrieve information. These will generally be lower-tariff questions and so remind pupils not to spend too long on their answers. Higher-tariff questions will ask pupils to comment on the 'how' questions about a piece of writing. They generally require pupils to comment how a particular atmosphere is created, or how a character is feeling. To answer these types of question effectively, pupils need to be trained in the habit of looking for 'clues' in text and using these to support their comments and analysis.

If pupils do not already have one, give them a glossary of literary techniques and devices. While terminology by itself won't gain pupils marks, it does act as a good shorthand when they write about text and makes their writing seem more sophisticated. Most important, however, is that pupils can identify and discuss *how* text works.

Rather than give pupils a whole extract to analyse, give them a piece of text which is broken into short chunks with no more than three questions on each section. You can use any text you feel suitable or, to make sure that the devices are readily available to pupils, you could write your own.

One way to introduce the idea is to base the text around a mystery or treasure hunt, with textual clues to be picked up throughout. This can help reinforce the idea of a 'search' rather than a cursory reading. For example:

Jason folded the piece of paper as small as he could and stuffed it in the secret compartment in the heel of his boot. He glanced down at its previous owner, still and white. 'Funny how they always look so peaceful afterwards,' he thought. Pausing for a moment, he washed his hands, put on some of the man's cologne and quietly closed the door.

o What has Jason just done? What made you think this?
o Has he done this before? What made you think this?
o Why do you think he did it? What made you think this?

Continue in the same vein, setting questions after small sections of text which encourage pupils to look for 'clues'. At least for the first few sections, ask pupils to stop after each section and share their answers so as to ensure that all are on the right track.

Some pupils' answers will be more detailed than others. They can be asked to go a stage further and look at why the 'clue words' led them to their conclusion.

Following on from this, pupils can look at a whole extract and focus on the specifics of a high-tariff question. Ask pupils to look closely at the question and any bullet points that may have been given as guidance, and underline the key words. They will use these words to structure their answer, using the bullet points as paragraph headings. They can then begin to structure their response in a number of ways. These could include underlining and annotating key words or phrases which could illustrate their answer. Remind pupils that they won't be able to write about everything and so to focus on specific examples and write about them in detail. Pupils could also make tables with headings such as 'device' and 'effect created' and 'What x does' or 'What this shows us'; or you could give pupils parts of sentences to fill in with observations or quotations.

The formula used by many to structure responses of this kind can be an efficient base. It has many names: PEE – Point, Evidence, Explanation; SEC – Statement, Evidence, Comment; 'The Hamburger Method' and so on. They follow the same basic format: 'I think that Jason has killed someone before [point]. I think this because he says "they always look so peaceful" [evidence]. The word "they" suggests there has been more than one and "always" also suggests that he has seen more than one dead body.' [explanation]

These kinds of formulas are a good starting point to get pupils in the habit of justifying and explaining their answers. The problem is that in a long answer, the formula can become very repetitive and can limit some responses. Provide pupils with suggested phrases that they can use in their writing to avoid repetition.

Pupils read body language every day. We all recognize signs which let us know how someone is feeling before they have spoken a word. A closer examination of body language and what meaning we can read from it can be of great benefit to pupils as readers and writers of text.

Ask the class to stand and shake their limbs gently. When they hear you shout an emotion, they are to freeze in a pose which depicts that emotion. Call pupils' attention to any particularly good examples. This can be extended by, for example, individual pupils being given emotions to pose for the class.

Put pupils into pairs and give them a series of three or four emotions to split between them. These are to be acted out without noise as part of a sequence. Selected pairs can show their sequence to the class who guess the emotions being illustrated.

Next, give pupils a text extract that has spaces for body language to be added. Above each space, write the emotion that is to be presented through clues given by the body. Pupils complete the passage, selecting appropriate body language. The passage is then read through with volunteers filling the gaps with their selections. Pupils can then compile a dictionary of the body, giving examples of body language and possible meanings.

Exploring poetry

Some pupils (and teachers!) find that, while they may enjoy reading and writing poetry, writing *about* poetry is something of a chore, if not a total mystery. Pupils can be taught about some features of poetry such as rhyme, voice, rhythm, sound, structure and imagery through some gentle exercises such as the following.

Pupils are quite likely to be familiar with limericks, and they can be a useful starting point for understanding rhyme and rhythm. Display a limerick on the board, OHP or IWB in prose form and read it to the class as prose, taking no notice of rhyme or rhythm. Ask pupils if they noted anything wrong and then ask a volunteer to read it out again. The rhythm and rhyme of limericks seems to be embedded in most children and so you should have many volunteers for this. Ask pupils to write out the limerick in their books in the correct format. The next stage is to ask pupils to come up with a set of rules for limericks. These should include number of lines; rhyme scheme and rhythm, or number of beats per line. They may also come up with some ideas about content and tone, such as that the first line introduces a person; the next three set up a situation; the final line acts as a punchline, and that the tone is humorous. Pupils can then write their own limericks using the rules as a guideline. You may wish to give some further support in the form of line starters or ends.

Before pupils begin to work on more complex metrical patterns, a sound understanding of rhythm and how it can be created is needed. As an introductory task, play pupils two pieces of music of different rhythms – obvious choices may be a slow song outlining love 'gone bad', and a fast-pace anthem of defiance or joy. Rap music can be useful here as the vocal patterns are so clearly rhythmic. While pupils are listening to the music, ask them to write down any observations about rhythm and its connection to meaning that they can. Ask them to note if the rhythm changes at any point and why they think this happens; if any words or phrases are repeated; and if this repetition has a corresponding rhythm change.

To reinforce the idea of rhythm, ask pupils to tap along to a poem such as 'The Badger' by John Clare, which has a fast, insistent pace that mimics the chase described in the poem. With your guidance, ask pupils to comment on how the fast pace is created – word and line length, punctuation, sound and repetition. Pupils' observations should be noted on the board and on their own copies of the poem. Give pupils a short list of themes or subjects and ask them to decide what kind of rhythm or pace would be most suitable for each, with reasons for their decisions. It is important here that some links are made between structure and meaning.

Next, distribute two short poems that have quite different, and quite obvious, patterns. Read out each poem in turn, emphasizing rhythm. In pairs, ask pupils to work out how the rhythm is created, using their notes as guidance. Again, ask pupils to think about why a certain rhythm is used and how it influences or reinforces meaning. The poems selected will depend very much on the needs of the class. Some pupils will, at this stage at least, need to be given poems that are straightforward in structure with very clear links between form and meaning. Other pupils will need to be stretched by looking at poetry that has more complex, irregular or changing patterns.

INTRODUCING IMAGERY

Much of the work which deals with connotation, atmosphere and metaphor can be useful when looking at imagery in poetry. Simple tasks such as word substitution can provide pupils with a base from which to explore how meaning is produced and connections made. Introduce the idea that imagery helps to create a picture for the reader. Provide pupils with two pictures and a number of strips that have written on them descriptive images that relate to elements of the pictures. Ask pupils in pairs to attach the images to the pictures in the place they think most fitting. Pupils can share their ideas and give reasons for their choices. This can be developed by giving pupils sets of different images and asking them to draw the scene or character as they see it from the images given. Again, ask pupils to share their work and look at how the images created certain pictures.

'The Fly' by Walter de la Mare can be an excellent starting point for an examination of imagery in a whole poem. It is structured as a list of similes and can be used easily and effectively as a model. Firstly, read through the poem with pupils and give pairs of pupils one line to analyse. Ask them to consider what impression is being created by the simile. For example, a rosebud is compared to a bed, which emphasizes its softness to the touch. Write or display each line on the board and ask each pair to give their ideas for that simile. These can then be recorded on the class copy. Once this is completed, talk to the class about what similes do – provide a comparison that gives us a particular impression. Pupils can then write their own simile poem. Pupils can 'be' a fly and offer similes on things they may encounter, which are not included in de la Mare's poem. They can use his lines as direct models, using the line starters as their starting point, but offering different similes or they can imagine that they are flying in a plane looking down at the landscape. Pupils can then swap poems and write down the impression created by each simile.

Onomatopoeia and sound imagery can also provide pupils with a way into discussing poetry. Explain that poetry is often meant to be read aloud and that sound can, therefore, play a big part in the impression created by a poem. Display sets of onomatopoeic sounds and ask pupils to come up with what is being described. For example, 'buzz, rustle, buzz, shriek, buzz, thud, thud, slap, slap, shriek' – a wasp chasing someone.

Ask pupils to think about why certain sounds remind them of certain things. They can then come up with a list of sounds from, for example, a busy supermarket, a football match or a beach. Ask them to share their ideas, which can be used to create sound poems.

Pupils now need to focus on words which are not onomatopoeic, but which nonetheless create a particular sense impression. Remind pupils about alliteration and show them a selection of words that they have to pair up using alliteration as their guide. This can be extended by, for example, asking pupils to write lines of alliteration for each letter of the alphabet, or short alliterative poems. Next, ask pupils to write lines which use alliteration for a particular purpose, such as a lullaby or a pre-match team chant. Ask pupils to focus on the sounds they will use for each example – soft, sibilant sounds for a lullaby and harder consonant sounds for the chant, perhaps. Pupils can share and discuss their work, exploring the effects created by sound.

Pupils can then look closely at poems such as 'The Listeners' by Walter de la Mare, or 'Beach Music' by David Johnson, noting any links they could make between the sounds of the words and their meaning.

Directed activities related to text (DARTs), such as cloze exercises (text completion) and sequencing can be used to encourage pupils to explore meaning. These sorts of tasks can be used to check understanding at the end of a series of lessons on poetry or as introductory tasks. For example, give pupils copies of a poem with key words missing. Ask pupils to fill in the gaps with words they think most fitting. This can be used to explore extended imagery or single images as best suits the class. Pupils can then read their poems to the class and differences discussed. Sequencing can also be used effectively. Divide a poem into segments and distribute to the class. Ask pupils to re-assemble the poem using clues they may find in rhyme scheme, rhythm, image patterns and so on.

If writing an analysis is going to be an end task, it is important to give pupils a framework for a critical response to a poem. Give the sentence starters for the introduction and then paragraph plans that guide pupils to specific features. These plans can vary in level of support depending on the needs of the pupil. They can also be graduated – providing considerable support for the opening paragraphs and then less as the essay progresses. This encourages pupils to consider the poem as a whole, looking at how various features combine to create meaning. It also provides pupils with an introduction to the kind of essay they will be expected write as they progress through the Key Stages.

As its origins would perhaps suggest, the ballad can have mass appeal and is easy to remember. Give the class copies of a ballad, such as 'La Belle Dame Sans Merci' by John Keats or 'What has Happened to Lulu?' by Charles Causley, written in prose form and read aloud. Next, explain to pupils what a ballad is: simple story; originally passed on orally, and event-driven rather than contemplative.

Put pupils into pairs or small groups and give each the ballad in verse form, but cut into separate stanzas. Ask the pupils to sequence the ballad and then feedback to class. Once the class has agreed on an order, the ballad can be pasted to a piece of paper, large enough for pupils to annotate in their pairs. A class reading of the poem can be undertaken, perhaps using pupils to read out a stanza each. Ask pupils to consider the differences between the prose version and the ballad, discussing which they found most effective and why. Display a series of questions, some of which deal with content, but some which ask pupils to look at structure, such as the following:

o What is the story of the poem? (No more than two sentences.)
o What characters are in the poem? How do you feel towards them? Why?
o What do you think the mood or tone of the poem is? Why do you think that?
o Are any metaphors or similes used? What are they? What do they make you think of?
o Are any words or phrases repeated (refrain)? What are they?
o Where is it repeated? Is there a pattern?
o Why do you think it is repeated?
o Is the poem broken into stanzas? If so, are they the same length? Why do you think this is?
o Do any of the lines rhyme? Is there any pattern?

The list can be extended to include, for example, sound imagery, line length, rhythm and so on. As the list of questions may be rather long, it may be a good idea to give each pair one or two questions on which to focus. Each pair can then feedback their answer(s), which can then be annotated on the displayed copy of the ballad and on pupils' own copies.

Ask the class to imagine they are going to describe a ballad to an alien. What would they come up with? From this establish an agreed set of key features for ballads that can then be used to help pupils write their own. These should include features such as the following: straightforward story telling, four-line stanzas, refrains (repeated phrases), use of rhyme, rhythm and line length. Pupils can devise their own ballads with varying degrees of support. Some may need simply the agreed common features; others may need a story on which to base their poem, line starters and so on.

Other effective narrative poems to use at KS3 are 'The Highwayman' and 'A Case of Murder' by Vernon Scannell. 'The Highwayman' is a tale of passion and tragedy that has some very effective visual imagery. 'A Case of Murder' is similarly rich with imagery – both visual and aural – and has a slightly manic tone, which develops throughout the poem. Read through the chosen poem with the class and focus on key images and features. Next, ask them to storyboard it individually. Drawing is not the focus here, so stick figures can be used if necessary – what you are looking for is a visual sense of the poem. Put pupils into groups and ask them to look at each other's visual ideas. Pupils are then going to work on a performance of the poem. This can be very effective, but it does need to be managed well. Be sure that group dynamics are effective; if not, move pupils as soon as possible. Also, be sure that you are in an appropriate and safe space – it may be worth using the hall or a drama space for this activity.

Before pupils begin, give them guidelines to follow regarding working as a group. Also, give them ideas about how they can organize their performance effectively. They may choose to use a single narrator, or a variety of voices for different elements; they may wish to use the form of a news programme or a play as the basic structure; they need to think of how they are going to create atmosphere; particular images and sounds will need to be represented and so on. Each group is then to perform the poem. This can be used as a speaking and listening assessment piece, and is best if completed over a couple of lessons if pupils are going to get the most out of it. I have seen a very effective performance of 'A Case of Murder' as a mystery piece with armchair-seated narrator and sitting room set!

A focus on plays

GENERAL OVERVIEW

Pupils, including weaker readers, generally enjoy reading plays as a class. It may be the participatory aspect, the variety of voices, the short chunks of rehearsable reading or many other factors. This enjoyment needs to be capitalized on and directed if the reading of plays is to be as effective as it possibly can be. Many pupils are not familiar with the conventions of drama and the explicit differences between a play and a novel. The following suggestions are not specific to any particular play, but are instead, broad ideas that can be altered and adapted as appropriate. Some tasks in other sections – such as Idea 44 'Introducing the class reader'– can be used to enhance understanding. Hopefully, these tasks will develop pupils' ability to both read and watch plays with greater understanding and to write their own.

Distribute or display extracts from a selection of novels and plays and ask pupils to identify them as one of these text types. Mind-map the pupils' ideas regarding the differences between a play and a novel. These should include textual aspects, such as the way each is presented on the page or the type of words used (for example, novels will have more descriptive detail and can shift quickly from place to place), alongside ideas about purpose and form (characters names are written on the left-hand side and no speech marks are used).

The class can agree on five key differences, but be sure to guide their choices so as to ensure that important elements such as stage directions and set are included. Pupils can then list each difference alongside an explanation as to why the difference exists and what purpose it serves. For example, pupils may conclude that plays do not need to have as much description as novels because the audience can *see* characters and places. Pupils can share their thoughts.

Distribute a scene – from the play studied, another play or one devised by you – that has no stage directions whatsoever. Explain to the class what stage directions are and who they are for. In pairs, ask pupils to add stage directions to the passage that will influence the way in which the scene is performed. You can let pupils decide their own direction here or guide them. Stage directions should influence what actions are performed and how; how the stage and actors should look and how words are delivered. Each pair can swap their annotated extract with another pair who can then act out the scene following the stage directions. Having observed all or a selection of performances, pupils can write about two very different interpretations they have seen, noting how each was presented and how difference was created.

Distribute to pupils the key events of a play in continuous prose. Ask pupils to break the play up into scenes. They must indicate why they have made a scene division – what indicators suggested it or what effect it may have. This can lead to discussion about why most plays are divided into acts and scenes, and pupils can write two sentences explaining their thoughts on the subject. If appropriate, they can also offer their opinions as to why some plays are structured without scene divisions.

Stage directions aside, pupils will need to understand other clues to expression which can be found in text. This does not apply exclusively to plays, but is especially useful here as their voices will be heard. Display lines which contain expression indicators such as question marks, exclamation marks and italics, such as:

Pat: So I'm going to the party?
David: You *do* have one for sale after all.
John: She's gone to town!

Pupil volunteers can read each line, putting in the expression suggested by the expression indicator. Next, display the same lines, but with different indicators used, such as:

Pat: So *I'm* going to the party.
David: You do have one for sale after all!
John: She's gone to town?

Again, volunteers can read the line with appropriate expression. Remind pupils that if they have lines coming up in a reading of a play and feel unsure, they can read a little ahead and rehearse their line in their head.

CLUES TO EXPRESSION

To reinforce or re-establish ideas about the differences between plays and prose, ask pupils to transform a scene into prose. Be sure that pupils are aware of the differences beyond simply putting a character's name in the margin. Characters and setting will have to be provided through description; speech marks will have to be used when characters speak; body language will be provided in prose and an omniscient narrator can describe how characters are feeling.

Similarly, pupils can put their knowledge about plays into practice by producing a playscript of their own. This can be based on a class reader; a given situation; be a 'missing' scene or alternative ending to the class play and so on. Again, pupils need to be reminded of the key features of a playscript and some will need starting lines or a model on which to base their own script. Remind them that the actors will have only their words to direct them and so they need to think carefully about the impression they wish to create. Pupils can perform their pieces if practical and appropriate.

Pupils can produce montages/posters which represent either the play as a whole, or particular scenes or acts. Each montage needs to include images that illustrate key themes, events or issues and a selection of words/phrases that are integral to the act/scene/play. The design of the montage should be in keeping with the tone of the play. If appropriate, groups can each be allocated a different key scene to illustrate as a montage and these can be used as an effective class display.

Before a word has been read or a theme introduced, pupils will have an opinion on the prospect of studying a Shakespeare play. Many of those opinions will be negative – making a daunting task seem even more hard work. It is, however, worth remembering that those feelings are more often than not based in a fear that the language will prove too difficult. As such, it is often useful to familiarize your class with Shakespearean language before they tackle a play. Some of these tasks will be more suitable for your class than others and some may need to be adapted in order to be effective.

A simple starting block is the use of the pronouns 'thee', 'thy', 'thou' and 'thine'. Give pupils simple sentences to translate such as:

I will take you shopping.
I will take thee shopping.

Your bedroom needs tidying.
Thy bedroom needs tidying.

You went skating.
Thou went skating.

Note that 'thee' is used when 'you' is the object; 'thou' when 'you' is the subject.

Pupils often find this curious hybrid of Shakespearean and contemporary English fairly amusing, which is a good icebreaker if nothing else.

Before reading the play give your pupils one or more of the following three tasks.

Give pupils a piece of Shakespearean text to read. This may be an extract from the play they are to study, or an unrelated piece of Shakespeare's work such as a sonnet. What is most important is that it is manageable, yet stretching. Read through the extract with the class and, in pairs, ask them to work out what it means. During class feedback, focus on any images or words that the class may struggle with. Once meaning has been agreed, ask the class, again in their pairs, to rewrite the extract in more modern English.

Pupils could undertake a guided research project on Shakespeare and his times. This helps pupils gain a richer understanding of elements of the plays which could otherwise make little sense. This can also be used to assess pupils' writing of information texts. As an introduction, ask pupils to offer any information they may already know, outline key facts and then give pupils a plan outlining sections you wish to be included.

Most pupils will be at least vaguely familiar with the story of many of Shakespeare's plays. Ask them to mind-map their ideas on the board. Pupils can then try to reduce their ideas to three key facts. If the class is studying *Romeo and Juliet*, show pupils the prologue and ask them to rewrite it in their own words.

Many teachers find that their classes gain deeper understanding, at least initially, if the play is re-figured in a more contemporary setting. While the adage that Shakespeare's stories are timeless may well be true, for many pupils this is obscured by the difficulty they experience in understanding the language. Put the plays into a different context which can be more readily understood by pupils. For example, *Macbeth* could be a based on a football team, a successful company or gangland power struggles; *Romeo and Juliet* can be transposed to supporters of rival football teams or gangs (you could show them the film of *West Side Story* to illustrate this fact. See Idea 72 for more on using film in the classroom). This can be undertaken as an introductory task, where the story is presented in more modern form and themes, and characters and feelings are discussed. Alternatively, pupils could write their own modern version, individually or in pairs, after reading the play.

As another way into the play emphasize the importance of opening scenes and what they can tell an audience about the play to come. If studying *Romeo and Juliet*, look at the opening scene and split the class in half, with one half taking the role of the Montagues and the other half the Capulets. If practical, let the class leave their seats and face each other as they say their lines. If suitable, the class can be seated along Capulet/Montague lines for the duration of their study of the play. If *Macbeth* is being studied, focus on the witches and what an audience may guess about the play based on the opening scene.

FOCUSING IN ON THE PLAY

Below are three ideas for getting your pupils engaged further with the plays.

Romeo and Juliet, along with other plays such as *A Midsummer Night's Dream*, is littered with insults. Collect the insults together as a table and ask pupils to write in the empty column what they think the insults mean. If need be, you can provide a list of insults along with translations which the pupils have to pair up. If appropriate, ask pupils to discuss the effect of the insults – what is being picked up on? What may that tell us? What kinds of words are used? How do they sound?

Select two key extracts, one of which shows, for example, the language of love and the other the language of hate. Ask pupils to make detailed, guided comparisons, looking at types of image used, punctuation, sound and so on. Pupils can then select a line or image from each that they find most successful and write three lines explaining why they found it so effective. These can then be made into illustrated 'image maps' of the play, whereby key images from each scene are illustrated alongside the appropriate quotation.

Groups can be allocated a character that they will focus on, either for the duration of the play or for specific scenes and tasks. In *Romeo and Juliet*, for example, the characters of Tybalt, Benvolio, Mercutio and Romeo could be allocated to specific groups who track their characters during the pivotal fight scene in Act 3. Each group then feeds back to the class, using apt quotations to back up their observations of their character's actions, intentions and thoughts.

Use film and music as tools to enhance learning. Film can be a valuable asset in the classroom, but it needs to used effectively. Simply sitting the class in front of the television for two lessons is not the most efficient use of time. Pupils often benefit more from seeing selected extracts, always shown with the understanding that what is shown is an interpretation rather than a definitive version. Ask pupils to comment on the presentation offered, what is revealed or explored, how characters are represented, any differences between the play and the film and so on. If possible, use a variety of different versions to enable pupils to compare and also to avoid them associating the play so closely with one film version. For example the 'Romeo shoots Tybalt after the car chase' and similar such comments that frequently pepper essays.

Play appropriate background music quietly when key scenes are being read or just before. This can help set the atmosphere and make the scene more memorable for many pupils. Pupils can also select their own soundtrack for selected scenes using music provided by you. Give pupils a list of scenes and ask them to write which piece of music is most fitting for a given scene, along with the reasons behind their selection.

Pupils should be made aware of key themes, images, etc. throughout the play. Create image, character and theme logs – on separate pages – which are filled in throughout the play. The way in which these are organized will vary from class to class, with some perhaps identifying and recording key features, while others may offer varying levels of analysis. Some understanding of features such as the aside and the soliloquy, and conventions such as tragedy and comedy would be beneficial to many pupils. Close reading of key scenes with graduated comprehension questions will, of course, be an invaluable strategy.

Select a scene and ask the class to provide detailed directions for actors. Split the class into groups, allocate each member a role – character or director – and give them 10 minutes to rehearse their scene. Each group can perform their scene, and the class can then comment on the performance, asking questions about directing decisions and commenting on what they found most effective.

At the end of the play, set up an inquiry into the tragic events that have occurred. Put pupils into groups and allocate them roles. Pupils then prepare the defence of the character and the part they played in the tragedy. If necessary, provide pupils with role-specific sheets with key scenes and information, which will help them prepare their role. Each group will need a defence and prosecution. Each group can then perform their role-play. This is a very effective task, which can focus pupils very keenly on a character's actions and intentions. This works equally well for many plays, for example *Macbeth*.

Similarly, other drama conventions can be used very effectively, such as hot seating; tableau and thought tracking. These are outlined in more detail in Section 10, Drama in the English classroom.

The ubiquitous newspaper front page is also effective when studying Shakespeare. The sensational nature of the plays' events lends itself to news stories. Pupils can collect information throughout the reading of the play and use it to construct their news story. Ask them to focus on what sort of angle their story is going to have; which characters they may have comments from; and which incidents are going to feature most prominently.

Non-fiction

This is a handy grid that can be used either as an introductory task or as a revision task. It is by no means definitive, but is a solid base upon which to build. Leave a variety of spaces blank, depending on where the grid is to be placed in a sequence of lessons, and ask the class to fill them in. Ask your class to add another column that will list possible audiences for each type.

Some of these text types are looked at in more detail in the next few pages.

Text type	Purpose	Layout	Style
Formal letter	To inform; persuade; explain.	o Date and address o Introduction o Content paragraphs o Signing off	o Dear Sir/Madam o Yours faithfully o Dear Mr/s o Yours sincerely o Standard English and a variety of sentence types used
Brochure/ leaflet	To persuade; inform.	o Heading/slogan o Illustration o Bullet points or short chunks of text o Contact information	o Use of exaggerated or emotive language and personal pronouns
Newspaper report	To inform.	o Headline o By-line o Introductory paragraph summarizing story o Paragraphs in columns o Direct quotation o Photograph	o First person not used except in direct quotation o Use of proper nouns
Report	To inform; recommend; discuss.	o Title o Introductory paragraph o Sub-headings o Conclusion/ recommendation	o Logical structure o Lack of personal pronouns o Use of passive/ objective tone
Advertise-ment	To persuade.	o Slogan o Illustration o Logo	o Persuasive language used o Personal pronouns often used

As is the case with most analysis of text, becoming familiar with the ways in which various text types work serves to inform pupils' own writing as well as their reading and understanding. While visual image still plays a significant role in the effect created by a newspaper article, the emphasis is much more on the effects created by features of language.

Distribute to pupils three versions of the same story. One version is to be written as a front-page newspaper story, while the others may be prose, a diary entry, a letter or any other type of text you feel would be most fitting. Ask pupils to identify which one is the newspaper story, writing five reasons for their decision on their copy of the story. These will include elements of layout in the main, such headline, columns, image and so on. Pupils can then feed back to class. Next distribute three texts which have the layout of a newspaper front page. Again, the subject can be the same, but ensure that only one is written in the *style* of a newspaper. The differences between the three can be subtle or quite obvious, depending on the needs of your class. Read each piece of text to the class and ask them to again identify which they think is the newspaper story.

The results may be more mixed this time. Ask pupils to give reasons for their choice and record any correct observations on the board. If possible display a class copy of the actual news story and use this to record a guided annotation. Distribute a simple glossary of terms and features to the class and read through it. Ask pupils to identify five features from the list which can be found in the front page. Pupils can then feed back to class and observations should be noted on the class copy. Some features may be more difficult to identify and will require guidance. Features to identify may include: features of headline such as alliteration, pun or rhyme; any use of the passive voice or tentative language; absence of first-person pronouns except in direct quotation; opening lines outlining story; sequencing of story (often shifts between past, present and future rather than following chronologically); adjective use; and ways in which people are identified by name, age, appearance, job and so on. While you will be guiding pupils' observations, try to ensure that it is their responses that are recorded rather than yours.

Distribute a copy of a tabloid front-page story to the class and display to the class a list of terms, such as headline, caption, byline, columns and so on. Firstly, ask pupils to label the front page using these terms. On a display copy, label the front page using pupils' responses. Next, distribute a broadsheet front page – covering the same story if at all possible. Pupils can again label the front page and then move onto filling in a grid such as the one below.

Ask pupils to consider the type of vocabulary used; tone; adjective use; sentence length; and types of headline. These can be recorded as comprehension answers or in a table.

Give pupils a selection of events and ask then to write front-page articles about the same story for both a tabloid and a broadsheet newspaper.

	Number of stories on front page	Size of headline	Number of words in headline	Size of image	Proportion of page covered in text
Tabloid					
Broadsheet					

INTRODUCING AUDIENCE AND PURPOSE

Bring in a selection of coloured print advertisements that are designed to appeal to a variety of audiences. Ask pupils in groups to fill in a simple table, such as the one opposite. Try to ensure that pupils focus not simply on what is being advertised, but rather on how the product is being presented. Pupils feed back to the class and then are set questions that encourage them to comment on, for example, what features are made to stand out by use of bold or large type, what colours are used and why and so on. Also, select key words or phrases from the advertisements and ask pupils to discuss what response they are meant to elicit. Are personal pronouns used? Flattery? What is being offered if you buy this product?

Pupils can then put all of this into place by writing a short advertisement of their own. They are to imagine that they are writing a full-page advertisement, with illustrations, for inclusion in 'Pen Pal Monthly'. Their aim is to attract as many replies as possible, without telling any lies! They can, however, present the truth in a more flattering way; for example, 'noisy' could become 'chatty' or enthusiastic'. They can use any illustrations or fonts they think will be most effective in creating the impression they want to make. Structure will need to be considered. Are they going to start with their best points? Will they write a long paragraph or smaller chunks of text? Are headings going to be used?

Pupils will need to consider what kind of pen pal they are hoping to attract and use this to help inform their advertisement. Once completed, pupils can swap their advertisements and write down an analysis of one another's work, looking at what impression was created, how that impression was created and what elements were most and least effective.

	What is being advertised?	What is the main image used?	What other visual features are used e.g. font type and size, colour, etc.?	What sort of language is used?	Who would this advert appeal to?	Why?
1						
2						
3						
4						
5						

Advertisements are a common feature of the everyday life of most pupils. They will be familiar with the *purpose* of the form – to persuade – and many will have some idea of the intended *audience*, which will need just a little teasing out. What many have a difficulty with is making the leap into understanding explicitly *how* an advert works. The following tasks can be used as appropriate and adapted to suit your class. It can be useful to break the various devices employed in advertisements into two types – language based and visual. Most pupils will more readily analyse the visual aspects of an advert and it is, therefore, helpful to begin with those elements.

Distribute a variety of visual images and ask pupils to write down their immediate response. Ask them to note down reasons for that response under headings such as colour, content, composition and so on. Next, display some phrases written in an incongruous font, such as:

Thieves steal Christmas presents

Super fun for teens

Ask pupils to select which phrase goes best with which font. Pupils can feed back to the class, giving reasons for their answers. Guide them towards ideas of purpose and audience.

Speaking and listening

Speaking and listening is not, in practice, a discrete curricular element, easily separated from reading or writing. These strands are, most frequently, all to be found in the same lesson and skills in one area often inform those in another. It is, for example, sometimes hard to differentiate firmly between the well-written speech and the well-delivered one, and some find it odd that a written essay can be a piece of a reading assessment. It remains the case, however, that assessment of speaking and listening is a feature of KS3 and KS4 PoS. It is also the case that in a busy timetable, the assessment of speaking and listening is not always prioritized. This is a real shame as not only is it the case that these lessons can appeal to many pupils, but these skills may be the ones most utilized in the outside world.

Some tasks that would be well placed as speaking and listening assessment pieces are outlined in other sections – the Shakespearean courtroom in Idea 99, for example. A few further suggestions are outlined below. As they are ideas for assessment, it is important that pupils have been explicitly *taught* the skills and features of effective verbal communication in a variety of situations and for a variety of purposes. This will include features such as body language; vocabulary choice; rhetorical devices; effective use of voice; techniques of persuasion and so on.

This type of exercise is doubtless a familiar feature of team-building training. It is very effective as an assessment of skills of group work, persuasion, problem solving and decision making, that pupils of all levels of ability find enjoyable and get a great deal out of.

Differentiation can be achieved through adding extension problems such as a group member who has a broken leg, or a river that needs to be crossed and so on. This task has also been used as the stimulus for a variety of writing tasks from the diary to the newspaper report.

Put pupils into groups of four and present them with the background story of the task, such as that their group has crash landed in the rainforest. Their small plane is wrecked and cannot be repaired. They do not know how long they will be lost, nor the location of the nearest town or village. Each group selects from a list provided by you a number of items they wish to take to help them on their journey. They can only take items up to a certain weight limit and must, therefore, think carefully about their decisions. For example:

○ 3 × blankets	4 weight units each
○ 1 × flare gun	3 weight units
○ 1 × box of waterproof matches	1 weight unit
○ 1 × 6ft square tarpaulin	3 weight units
○ 5 × 5ltr water containers (full)	5 weight units each
○ 3 × machetes	3 weight units each
○ 1 × 12ft rope	4 weight units
○ 100 × painkilling tablets	1 weight unit
○ 1 × gas camp stove (full)	2 weight units
○ 1 × book 'Edible Plants'	2 weight units

The list needs to be longer than this so as to give pupils real choice, but the above is a start. Limit their choices to around 28 or so weight units. Monitor each group as they make decisions and then ask each group to present their choices to the class, giving reasons for their decisions. This can be continued by then giving the groups a problem to solve using just those items they have elected to take with them.

This can be used in a variety of ways and is a good individual assessment piece. While persuasive language will be the focus, other elements, such as presenting in formation, can also be features. The basic premise is that each pupil is given an identity, and then has to prepare and present a short talk justifying their place in the hot-air balloon. For example, occupational categories can be used so that a dentist, child minder, baker or bus driver may have to persuade the class of their use to the group. Other background stories can be used, such as a new society being set up on a remote island, but the premise remains the same – each pupil persuading the others they are indispensable.

This task can be used in a variety of ways and in a variety of groupings. As can be surmised, it tests pupils' abilities to give instructions. Pupils are told to imagine that they have been asked to instruct an alien – who has a basic grasp of English conveniently enough – to make a cup of tea; walk to a given point in the room/school/ locale; make toast; buy a drink and so on. If possible, arrange the task so that 'the alien' (perhaps you!) physically follows the instructions as they are given. Try to be as literal in your responses to the instructions given as possible so as to reinforce and test the ability to be clear and unambiguous when instructing.

THE INSTRUCTOR

THE INDIVIDUAL TALK

The individual talk. This old stalwart is not very fashionable any more, although it certainly has its merits. It can be used to assess explaining and describing skills, depending upon the topics chosen. One of the benefits of this type of task is that it can be used to allow pupils a chance to talk about something that interests *them*. That said, it is still necessary for pupils to be given the skills so as to ensure that their talks have focus and engage their audience. This can be differentiated by applying further restrictions such as given audience or purpose, which can help focus more able pupils more keenly on matters such as tone or vocabulary.

Another idea is to use information and communications technology (ICT) as a presentational aid. Pupils can use PowerPoint, for example, to help focus their talks. If ICT is to be used, however, ensure that the focus remains on the talk rather than technical proficiency. Be sure to give time limits for talks and ask pupils to check topics with you before they begin to research. Too narrow a focus, such as Manchester City vs. Manchester United 1982, can make for a talk of limited appeal unless it is handled very skilfully.

Debate can be a very successful assessment piece and can be used to assess pupils' work in pairs or individually. It is important that pupils are aware of the rules governing debate if an all-out shouting competition is to be avoided. Firstly, introduce the notion of debate as distinct from argument. Then give pupils a set of simplified rules and explain that the debates will be governed by these. These rules should include:

a) The idea of a motion in the form 'this house believes that . . .'.
b) The roles of the people to be involved, which should be at least chair, proposer of motion and opposer of motion.
c) Strict time constraints, after which each speech must end. This can be altered depending on the class, but try not to make it too long.
d) The role of the audience as observer not participator. This can be relaxed in an *organized* question-and-answer session after the debate if you wish.
e) Outlines regarding the form of each speech.
f) A standard format for the debates, e.g. chair introduces the motion and each speaker; proposer's speech; opposer's speech; summing up by chair.

For a first debate at least, it may be an idea to give pupils the motion to be debated and whether they will be proposing or opposing. Depending on the class, you can also act as chair so as to ensure that the debates run smoothly. This sort of task can be differentiated in a number of ways such as topics to be debated; time limits; help with structure during preparatory stages and so on. Further elements can be added, too, such as 'points of information' during the speeches or 'out of the hat' unprepared debates. The rule-governed nature of the formal debate can, if prepared well, provide a challenge to the most able pupils and a guiding structure for those who may struggle with English.

STORY SHARING

This is a simple, short and sweet activity which tests pupils' listening abilities along with their ability to tell a story. Ask pupils to tell a partner an interesting, funny, scary, unusual or memorable story about themselves. This can fit in as part of a wider sequence of lessons based around autobiography or horror stories, for example. Pupils then take turns to retell their partner's story. Give time guidelines to this as some pupils will squash the story into two or three sentences, while others could happily fill the entire lesson up. Emphasize that they must retell the story in as interesting a way as possible, creating atmosphere as well as recounting information. This can be developed further by reading a short story or extract to the class which is written from one character's perspective, or which focuses on one character's feelings – for example, extracts from *Boy* by Roald Dahl or *About a Boy* by Nick Hornby. Pupils then retell the story from the point of view of one of the other characters.

Ideally, this group task will need a couple of lessons to be really effective. Split the class into interest groups of four or five. Depending on the scenario you choose, these could include teenagers; pensioners; environmentalists; parents and so on. Set a scenario for the class such as one of the following:

An improvement grant has been awarded to the local community and various groups are invited to submit bids.

A shopping mall is to be built in the local area and groups are invited to submit their views regarding location, suitability and so on.

The scenario and group identities can be varied to suit your class. Each group then submits a presentation which puts forward their proposal. This should also include reasons why the proposals which may be put by the other groups are less satisfactory. This task can be altered and embellished in many ways. For example, a devised location and scenario can be produced, using resources such as a map which identifies significant features such as preservation sites, local schools and hospitals.

THE PROPOSAL

THE AWARDS CEREMONY

This can be undertaken as a group or paired activity and helps to focus pupils on making and justifying choices. Groups or pairs are given a category, such as 'Best Female Singer'; 'Best Day-Trip Venue'; 'Best Meal in the School Canteen' or 'Best Christmas Song'. Pupils then have to decide the nominations and eventual winner of their category. During the discussion phase, all opinions have to be justified, rather than simply choosing a winner because the most dominant force in the group has decided. At an end-of-task 'awards ceremony', each group/pair announces the nominations and winner of their category and gives the reasons for their choice.

Thinking skills

As teachers we may sometimes feel that our lessons prioritize content over process, or that we have so much to cover that we don't stop to think about thinking. Lessons that provoke, stimulate and challenge pupils help pupils become creative and independent thinkers. Alongside the ability to decode and discuss, we need to find ways to encourage pupils to make connections, move from the specific to the general and back again, synthesize and transform information and skills.

Of course, thinking skills are part and parcel of most lessons. When we ask pupils to analyse or compare texts, to deduce what a character may do next or present an argument, we are asking them to use and develop their thinking skills.

In your planning, highlight those words connected with the kinds of thinking skills (analysis, synthesis, evaluation and so on) we want our pupils to engage with. Let pupils become familiar with these terms and use them in plenary and exposition. Give them the vocabulary of thinking and provide opportunities for your pupils to deduce, justify, transform and synthesize information and ideas.

Give pupils a short piece of text. This may be from a newspaper article or a piece of literature. What is important is that there are a set of fairly clear assumptions that could be drawn from the piece. For example, if you chose an extract from *Romeo and Juliet*, you could list assumptions underneath such as: young people don't think before they act; love is the most powerful emotion; secrets have bad consequences and so on. Pupils can then discuss the assumption they find most interesting as a whole class or group. The class can then come to agreement as to which, if any, of the assumptions they feel are less problematic. This sort of task invites pupils to examine what they know of a given text, while also thinking about what assumptions are, how we reach them, whether they have any value, how they can be examined, the place of the exception or of faulty logic and so on. This sort of task can be made more sophisticated by asking pupils to choose between assumptions that appear to be fairly similar. Continuing with the above example, this may include: people should stand up for what they feel no matter what the consequences; people should take consequences into account in order to make the best decision; people should learn how to play the system to get what they want and so on. This sort of task leads into debates about ethics as well as encouraging pupils to develop questions.

We often ask pupils to 'compare and contrast' in the English classroom, and we usually take it for granted that they can do this. Quite often what pupils are doing is simply listing differences, which is not quite the same thing. Being able to sort ideas and objects in this perhaps simple way is an important skill. It focuses pupils in on links and separations between objects, texts or ideas.

Display two quite different objects. They may be close to hand – a board pen and a book, for example – or specially selected for a specific purpose. Ask pupils to list similarities and differences. A Venn diagram can be used here or a table. Next, show pupils two or more objects that are similar in some ways but quite different in others – an apple and a tennis ball, for example. Discuss the differences and ask the class to categorize them into types of difference and similarity. These will include, for example, appearance, feel and function. (This can, of course, be done after the first 'compare and contrast' task.)

Pupils can then complete a diagram or list that enables them to see if objects are more like than unalike, based on different criteria. Other objects to compare may be a coin, a piece of glass and a diamond, for example. Pupils can then decide in pairs which comparison criteria they think is most important, why and if this is the case in all instances. Pupils may decide, for instance, that while a tennis ball might look more like an apple than a pineapple does, the pineapple is more similar to the apple as they are both fruit. Be sure that you give your pupils the vocabulary of comparison: the same, similar, but, because, however, unlike and so on.

These skills can then be applied to text. You can choose to give your pupils an information text about, say, species of dog, or British theme parks, and ask them to compare and contrast the types described within, or you could give them two texts (fiction or non-fiction) to compare. You can set categories/criteria for comparison or you can ask the pupils to explain these during their own comparisons.

Debates, dialogues and discussions are very useful tools in the classroom. As well as extending and developing speaking and listening skills, pupils are given the opportunity to explore ideas and opinions, as well as the chance to practise and enhance their skills of reasoning and working with other people. What is often left out in class discussion and debates is the listening component. This is a shame as not only is it a skill in itself and a social tool, it also means that all too often pupils are not really responding to others' viewpoints, but rather waiting for a gap in order to assert their own opinion. These kinds of response are, therefore, sometimes lacking in logical links or any understanding of other points of view, and become phatic assertions, rather than actual responses to the thoughts of another.

Distribute or display to your pupils a scenario based upon a disagreement. This may be, for example, parents/guardians forbidding their child from attending a party – you can elaborate and add detail as you see fit. Split the class into two and ask one half to jot down what they think the parents' objections might be, and the other to jot down the reasons the child may have for going. Pupils can then feed back – note their comments on the board. Next ask pupils in pairs or small groups to see if there are any links between any of the comments or any comments that they feel answer each other/cancel each other out and also indicating any common areas of concern – for example, both parties may have a desire for safety. Pupils can then feed back to the class, indicating where they feel an objection has been met with a valid reason. If the class agree, that objection can be crossed out. Similarly, if there is an area of common ground, this can be highlighted. Pupils will hopefully see that, often, differences of opinion do share common ground and also that some agreement can be reached through consideration of another's point of view.

LISTENING AND RESPONDING TO OTHERS

DEVELOPING LOGICAL ARGUMENTS

Once pupils have explored the idea that argument is not necessarily purely emotional, but rather has reasons and explanations, you can move pupils towards developing their logical responses.

Be sure that pupils have the vocabulary of logical argument: should, must, ought, necessarily, since, because, for, as, in as much as, for the reason that, first, therefore, hence, thus, so, consequently, it follows that, from this . . . and so on.

Give pupils a set of sentences such as the following:

All year 8 pupils are going on a trip.
Sam is in year 8.
               Therefore
Sam is going on a trip.

Discuss how the conclusion followed from the information given in the first two statements.

Next, ask pupils to fill in the gaps:

1) We always eat chips on a Friday.
2) _____
3) We will eat chips tomorrow.

1) All fish have fins.
2) My goldfish is a fish.
3) _____

Again, explore how the conclusions follow logically on from the two premises. Next, ask pupils in pairs to set each other these simple, three-line logic puzzles. If any don't work or cause argument, ask pupils to note down why. It will often be because one or both of the premises is faulty for one reason or another, for example:

1) Girls are better than boys
2) Halima is a girl and Jake is a boy.
3) Halima is better than Jake.

Ask pupils to write down what makes an argument logical and then agree a set of rules, which can be displayed.

Helping pupils develop an understanding of connections is an important part of English lessons. Exercises such as this can really help pupils focus more clearly on key aspects of a text or idea, and think about what links certain aspects.

Ask pupils to give you a word that they associate with a class reader they have just finished, or a short story they have just read. The words do not have to be plot-related at all, but simply the first word that comes to mind when the pupil thinks of the text (ask them not to use superlatives, as 'excellent' or 'rubbish' won't fit your purpose). Aim for around 20–30 words. Note these on your board and then ask pupils in small groups to decide on four or five categories into which they could place the words. A word can go into more than one category, but all words must be used. Pupils can add any words they feel important during the exercise. For example, pupils may choose the categories of 'Magic', 'Friendship', 'Good vs. Evil' and so on, for Harry Potter.

Circulate while pupils complete their category tables so as to ensure that pupils have not given themselves categories that are too narrow or limiting.

Pupils are then told that they have to prepare a presentation explaining their choices of category and their decisions. You can opt to ask pupils to present their findings as a poster if you wish, illustrating their key categories and ideas and then discussing them with the class.

This can be differentiated by, for example, providing pupils with a set of words printed individually on cards. You may also provide categories. Ask pupils to sort the words into the most appropriate category.

This sort of task asks pupils to differentiate clearly between words which are fairly similar in meaning. Not only does this allow for a discussion about how we understand words and how we use them, but it also moves pupils towards greater precision.

Give pupils pairs of words such as:

Confident/big-headed
Learn/know
Assertive/aggressive
Love/adore

Ask pupils to discuss in their pairs what they think the differences and similarities are between the words and then to come up with their own definitions for each.

Pupils can then listen to each other's definitions and agree on those which they feel most approporiate. If you wish, you can then use a dictionary to measure any differences.

WHAT'S THE DIFFERENCE BETWEEN . . . ?

Give pupils cards printed with, for example, key characters or important events from a studied text, school rules, moral standpoints, ingredients for a successful friendship and so on. In pairs or small groups, ask pupils to arrange these cards in rank order, justifying and debating about positioning. Pupils can then agree their order and present back to the class. It is useful to encourage dialogue here so as to afford pupils the chance to explore the ideas of others and justify their own. The class can then agree a whole-class order. This can, of course, be organized as a diamond or pyramid rather than a simple ascending line. The organizational shape you use brings with it its own organizational dilemmas and principles.

Give pupils cards printed with a number of events – these can be in word or image form. Again in pairs or small groups, ask pupils to arrange the events in a sequence that makes sense to them. You can also give out or display a number of connectives. Be sure that pupils are quite clear as to the relationship suggested by each connective, and ask them to connect each event using each connective once only. Pupils can then retell their version of events to the whole class. This can, in turn, be used as a plan for a piece of writing.

USING CARDS TO ENCOURAGE THINKING

Drama in the English classroom

This can be utilized effectively as a speaking and listening assessment, or as a way of exploring character. Both the pupil in the hot seat and the rest of the class need to have considerable knowledge of the character for this to be effective. A pupil assumes the role of a named character in, for example, a studied novel and answers questions from the class. While questions tend to be centred on information found in the text, the task can be extended to include broader questions and answers which are 'in character'.

If this type of task is to have real value, pupils need to understand that they are 'in character', and what this means. Events should not be the focus here. Pupils will need to prepare by exploring the character in great depth to show their understanding.

This is an effective (and quiet!) activity which helps pupils grasp a sense of situation and atmosphere, as well as an understanding of the role of body language in creating a particular impression. Essentially, tableau functions like a staged snapshot. Pupils are required to create a 'freeze frame' of a situation and hold it. The most effective of these will utilize, for example, different levels and create a real sense of the scene and reactions to it.

Pupils can produce tableaux of different key scenes for others to identify, or each group can produce tableaux of the same scene and note the differences.

TABLEAU

THOUGHT TRACKING

This one tests and develops skills of empathy. Here pupils act a scene and then freeze in tableau. Individual pupils are then selected to voice the thoughts their character may have at that particular point. It is less rigidly structured than hot seating and requires pupils to react quickly.

This type of activity requires students to react on the spot to events other than those in the text studied. Tableaux and thought tracking, just as the other drama techniques you can use in the English classroom, are not confined to text-related activities but can be used to explore character, situation, style and so on as part of a focus on language.

ROLE-PLAY

The old favourite! Role-play can be used in a variety of classroom situations and can be used to explore elements of the curriculum connected to both language and literature. Pupils adopt a role and interact with one another, exploring the limits and qualities of their given role and its attendant viewpoint. For example, a courtroom scene can be used just as effectively to explore issues of blame in *Romeo and Juliet* as to provide a convincing framework for a debate on school-leaving age. As a language-based exercise, put pupils into small groups and give them a card with a situation and list of suggested characters. Pupils can then write their own short plays based on the information given. Be sure to direct them to focus on how the play will begin and end; how each character will feel; how this is to be represented in both words and actions and any drama techniques they may wish to include. If possible, ask each group to consider ideas for set and costume and to have reasons for their choices. This can be assessed as a voice performance or, if time and space allow, as a play. Pupils can also create their own news programme based on a literary text or as a language exercise. Ensure that the different elements of the programme, such as weather report, local news, studio presenters and outside reports are included; and that differences in tone, language and so on are noted.

ICT and English

As you are no doubt aware, the national curriculum orders for English outline the subject-specific requirements for the use of information and communications technology (ICT) as part of the teaching and learning of English. Statutory requirements aside, ICT can be a massively successful and, yes, exciting aid in the English classroom, both as a presentational tool and as an interactive learning aid. However, it is important to remember that not all lessons will be better off delivered using PowerPoint or the IWB, and that ICT is used most effectively when it is used as a resource, not as the lesson itself The following ideas provide some pointers for those who have yet to have the opportunity to explore the possibilities afforded by ICT in the English classroom.

That the Internet is an invaluable research tool for pupils and teachers alike goes without saying. What needs to be remembered is that the Internet alone is simply a tool, and its effective use in the classroom requires specific guidance and aims. The too-easily available plethora of coursework essays and unsavoury websites aside, Internet research can end up as an inefficient trawl through endless pages with little actual focus. Try putting 'Shakespeare' into a browser and the million-plus pages that come up can be daunting to say the very least. When using the Internet with a class, the same rules should apply as they would to any lesson – clear and specific aims and objectives should be the sustained focus.

For example, to maintain the focus of the class and help keep their twitchy fingers away from games and ring tones, give pupils *specific* websites to search for *particular* information. If you are researching Shakespeare, have a very specific focus – his life, or the Globe Theatre, for example – and arm your pupils with the addresses of websites you have already checked for suitability, and task sheets that can only be completed using information found on directed websites. This also allows for differentiation as pupils can be directed to different sites and search for information of varying degrees of complexity. Be sure, too, that the information is then *used* for a purpose – group presentations or comprehension, for example – rather than being an end in itself. There is sometimes a tendency for lessons such as these to be a little lacking in direction and, therefore, real purpose. The Internet cannot take the place of a well-planned lesson. What it can do is provide an effective resource for that well-planned lesson to succeed.

DRAFTING AND EDITING

Word-processing packages can enable pupils to edit and re-sequence text efficiently. This in turn can enable pupils to make editing decisions which explore style, meaning and structure. Texts can be transformed to meet the needs of different audiences and purposes, and spelling and grammar checks can help improve accuracy. This is not to suggest that word-processing is not without its problems. Often, pupils use word-processing simply to produce a 'best' copy of an essay or piece of work. While this may sometimes be unavoidable, it is not the most efficient use of ICT. The real worth of word-processing lies in its flexibility. Pupils should use ICT to enable them to re-draft and edit meaningfully, rather than simply as a typewriter. This can be practised by, for example, giving pupils sequencing or editing tasks as part of their study of a text. Pupils need to be made aware of the limitations of spelling and grammar checkers. While these features are valuable tools, they do not do away with the need for accurate spelling. Many spelling mistakes, especially of words that sound alike, may not be picked up. Word-processing can also be used effectively in the creation of collaborative texts, where groups of pupils construct a text as a combined effort. This will mean saving and retrieving work from common folders, but it can be very effective.

Packages such as Publisher can be very effective in enabling pupils to gain deeper understanding of how certain types of text work. They provide pupils with the means to transform texts and to produce work which is well presented and in keeping with text type. Pupils can produce a newspaper front page based on a Shakespeare play, create a leaflet for a local attraction or an advert, using images and text. As with any tasks of this nature, the focus must remain on the learning objective for English. Ensure that pupils are well furnished with sufficient knowledge about the texts they will transform and create before they begin.

Presentational tools such as PowerPoint can be very effective in the classroom. As a teacher, you can present ideas and key points clearly and without turning your back to the class. Many pupils respond well to the use of image, colour and sound that is available in presentations of this kind. Avoid using too much writing in your presentation – key points should be flagged up with further information provided through talk. PowerPoint can be used interactively, too. Clicking on the barely visible triangle that presents itself on the bottom left-hand corner of each slide enables you to change the pointer to a pen. This can be used by you or by pupils to annotate text, add punctuation and so on. The IWB can allow pupils to interact with text in an immediate and creative way. Pupils can sequence texts; design sets for plays; look at video clips of plays while reading text or questions; create professional-looking adverts; annotate extracts as a class; listen to speech while completing exercises on accent and dialect – the possibilities are endless. The IWB allows pupils to transform, create, explore, organize, analyse, modify and model a wide range of text types.

Boys and English

GENERAL POINTERS

The debates continue to rage as to the extent, nature, cause, cure and, indeed, even the actual existence of the achievement gap between boys and girls. Debates aside, English, whatever the reasons may be, is the core subject where boys regularly do less well than girls. Years of research and initiatives have yet to find conclusive answers or reasons for this, and it has to be noted that factors beyond the classroom are generally out of our reach. Nonetheless, some strategies seem to help. It is difficult to deal with as complicated and far-reaching a topic as this in so few words and more difficult still to do so without lapsing into stereotype, cliché and superficiality – all of which I doubtless employ in the following tips. It must also be noted that many of the suggestions that follow may be elements of a successful lesson per se, rather than one aimed specifically at boys.

The effective and guided use of ICT in the English classroom seems to have a marked effect on boys' attitudes to tasks. Where possible and appropriate, try to include ICT as a meaningful part of your lessons. As well as using ICT to present aspects of your lesson to the class, give pupils the opportunity to use ICT themselves. PowerPoint presentations can be given by pupils; newspapers created using Publisher; effective editing and redrafting can be undertaken; Internet research; and interactive lessons with the IWB can be undertaken.

SHORT AND SHARP

Organizing lessons as a series of short, timed tasks is effective in maintaining focus. Where possible, build up to the overall aim of your lesson through timed, directed activities which last for no more than 10 minutes. Also, start lessons as soon as pupils enter the classroom. Have lesson starter sheets ready or have a short exercise written on the board before pupils arrive. Remind pupils of the aims of individual tasks and of the overall lesson. Pupils respond well when given the opportunity to understand why they are doing something – boys in particular.

It has been found that many pupils and boys in particular, respond to the organization of lessons around the number **five**. This can include, for example: the five-part lesson; being asked to list five facts about a given topic; having 5-minute tasks as a part of lessons; five paragraph plans; five questions and so on. While this sounds quasi-mystical, it is a surprisingly effective organizing principle. Perhaps five is a number which allows for a certain degree of engagement without being daunting and off-putting.

FIVE

Given that boys as a group are less likely to read in their spare time than girls, text selection can really matter. It is a cliché too far to suggest that boys only like to read action-packed stories with violent episodes and little discussion of feelings. Nonetheless, boys will tend to enjoy (or allow themselves to enjoy) certain types of texts more than others. For example, a book such as *The Outsiders* by S. E. Hinton can be a tremendously successful book with boys – particularly at KS3, even though it is, perhaps, quite dated and deals with emotional issues. It does have male protagonists and despite its essentially moral tone, depicts the lifestyle of, and sympathizes with, 'rebels'.

Many schools have implemented a boy-girl seating plan for English lessons and found this to be effective. It seems to disperse 'pack' elements and tendencies, amongst both boys and girls. While this may not be appropriate for every class and every lesson, it may well be worth using for certain tasks.

Other seating plans can also be implemented, of course gender isn't the only organizing principle you may consider.

Differentiation

Differentiation is a vital element of your teaching if all pupils are to meet their various potentials. It is also one of the most time-consuming and complicated, and sometimes takes a back seat to the many other pressing demands. Even if pupils are in sets for English, there may still be a surprisingly wide range of abilities within the group, of a general or more specific nature.

In order to address this issue effectively, the starting point should be a survey of available data on pupils. This can include SAT results, IEPs or ILPs, CAT scores, reading-test results; information from primary schools, LSAs and other teachers and so on. While it is unrealistic to expect each teacher to undertake an exhaustive research project on each pupil, and this is more of a whole-school issue, do try to use whatever information is made available to you, as it does save time in the long run. You will also be your own best guide, as many problems can surface relatively quickly, either in class or when work is taken in. Idea 112 suggests strategies that you can try in the classroom depending on the needs of your pupils. Some are general strategies and some are aimed at more particular difficulties. They are rather broad, but should at least provide a starting point or a springboard for more individual support.

○ Avoid long-winded instructions. Try to make instructions clear, short and to the point, asking pupils to rephrase to check understanding. Do not give more than two instructions at a time.

○ Use your voice. Adopt different specific tones of voice for various aspects of your lesson such as instructing, explaining, reading and so on. It helps act as a verbal signpost.

○ Use writing frames and clear, structured worksheets to help support and structure writing. Provide models or sentence starters and break down longer tasks into shorter, more manageable stages.

○ Rather than simply start a class reader, ease pupils in by, for example: discussing its themes and making connections to pupils' own experiences or world; looking at the opening or another appropriate part closely, and checking understanding through frequent, guided questions and discussions to ensure that pupils are engaged.

○ Avoid over-reliance on writing. Visual learners respond well to illustrations, graphs, colour coding and so on, to record or remember ideas. Similarly, some pupils respond well to practical, 'doing' tasks and others prefer tasks which are based on speaking and listening. Try to include a variety of teaching and learning styles in your lessons.

○ When preparing worksheets and resources, try to make sure that your font is large and clear. Also, avoid overcrowding as this can obscure focus and lead to confusion.

○ Establish a regular organizational pattern covering aspects such as entrances and exits; seating arrangements; where work is kept; question protocol and so on. Within this basic framework, lessons can, and should, be varied, but a basic, established pattern helps pupils concentrate.

- Set questions which allow pupils to achieve something. For example, have some 'spotting' questions as part of comprehension exercises or allow those pupils who are least able to give their answers first in group activities. Perhaps frame questions so that they get progressively more difficult, or involve more sophisticated answers, and provide guidance and support or allow pupils to answer in pairs.
- Set regular, achievable, specific, short-term targets which can be monitored easily. Praise achievement when a target is met and have high expectations. Similarly, set tasks which pupils can complete in the time given.
- Don't be too reliant on the board. Many pupils find large chunks of board-writing difficult to follow. If this is unavoidable, try to use different colours to allow various elements to stand out more easily and enable pupils to find their place.
- Play to pupils' strengths. Once you have worked out what works best for your pupils, give them the chance to show what they can do rather than stick to formula simply because it feels more comfortable.

Below is some suggested reading on teaching English:

Getting the Buggers to Write: 2nd Edition – Sue Cowley,
    Continuum 2004
A practical guide to improving students' writing skills
in the classroom.

Getting the Buggers to Read – Claire Senior, Continuum
    2005
Practical guide showing how teachers can improve their
students' reading skills.

Teaching Poetry – Fred Sedgwick, Continuum 2003
Fred Sedgwick shows how meaningful the relationship
between reading and writing poetry can be and how it
can open the creative minds of young people.

101 Red Hot English Starters – Simon Adorian, Letts
    Educational Ltd.
This is aimed at students between 11 and 14 and
essentially does what it says on the tin.

Jumpstart! Literacy Games – Pie Corbett, David Fulton
    Publishers Ltd 2003
Contains literacy starters and warm-up games, which are
practical to use. Also contains photocopiable material.

Teaching Shakespeare – Rex Gibson, Cambridge
    University Press 1998
Practical guide to teaching Shakespeare in schools.

English Teaching in the Secondary School – Mike Fleming
    and David Stevens, David Fulton Publishers Ltd
    2004
A guide to English teaching, which covers all the main
components.

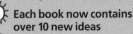